# Business Reports in English

# Business Reports in English

Jeremy Comfort
Rod Revell
Chris Stott

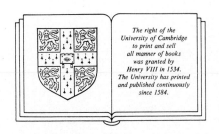

The right of the
University of Cambridge
to print and sell
all manner of books
was granted by
Henry VIII in 1534.
The University has printed
and published continuously
since 1584.

## Cambridge University Press
Cambridge
New York   New Rochelle
Melbourne   Sydney

Published by the Press Syndicate of the University of Cambridge
The Pitt Building, Trumpington Street, Cambridge CB2 1RP
32 East 57th Street, New York, NY 10022, USA
10 Stamford Road, Oakleigh, Melbourne 3166, Australia

© Cambridge University Press 1984

First published 1984
Reprinted 1987

Designed by Andrew Weall and Associates

Printed in Great Britain
at the University Press, Cambridge

Library of Congress catalogue card number: 84–1890


*British Library cataloguing in publication data*

Comfort, Jeremy
Business reports in English.
1. English language – Business English
2. English language – Text-books for foreign
speakers
3. Business report writing
I. Title   II. Revell, Rod
III. Stott, Chris
808'.066651021      PE1128

ISBN 0 521 27294 7

MX

# CONTENTS

# DEDICATION

To Chris Stott, tragically killed in September 1981, whose idea this book was and who did much of the ground work.

# ACKNOWLEDGEMENTS

We would like to thank our colleagues at York Language Training Ltd who gave us the time and space to complete this book, and particularly Trish Stott for her help in proof reading and for her critical eye.

The authors and publishers would like to thank the following people and teaching centres for their help in piloting this material, and for providing valuable feedback before publication:

David Ward-Perkins, Acces, France
Sheila Sirey, Communications in Business, France
Jim Corbett, Key English Language Services, Sweden
Linda Baker, Kodak-Pathe, France
Jon Leckey, ARAMCO, Saudi Arabia
Malachy Scullion, Saudi Arabian Airlines, Saudi Arabia
Henricus Verweijen, SPIDI, Austria

# TEACHER'S INTRODUCTION

## USES OF THE COURSE

*Business Reports in English* is designed for two target groups who need or will need to read and write business reports:
1 Practising managers and secretarial personnel in fields such as administration, export, finance, general business, marketing, personnel and production.
2 Business studies students.
The entry level for both groups is intermediate to upper-intermediate.
The course can be used in the classroom and/or for self-study. It is sequentially ordered and therefore should be worked through from the beginning. It can be used as:
1 A main course in report reading and writing.
2 A supplementary component of a general business English course.
If students have to deal with specialised reports in their jobs, *Business Reports* can be used for the core of the course with students supplying examples from their own work for study alongside this book. In this way the teacher can point out the parallels between the principles exemplified in this book and the students' specific needs as applied to their jobs.

## DESIGN OF THE COURSE

The course teaches the skills of report reading and writing using a system of organisation applicable to any native speaker report writer. Thus the unit headings reflect the logical steps in writing a report, from 'Collecting the information' through to 'Summarising' and 'Appendix'.
The underlying methodology of the course is that the students should be presented with task-oriented activities that are both challenging and authentic in the field of business. Using this approach, the student is taken through the following stages in each unit:
1 He or she is forced to read and think about the *content* of the report or extract.
2 He or she has to think about the *structure* and *organisation* of a report.
3 He or she has to think about the *language* used to express the content.
4 He or she has to apply this knowledge to the skill of *writing* a report.
The extracts from the reports have been adapted from authentic sources (company reports, project reports, personnel reports, etc.) and selected to represent certain business areas (see Contents).

# COURSE ORGANISATION

There are six units, an appendix, a key and a glossary.

## Units 1–6

### 1 Reading and understanding

The student is required to read a number of report extracts which exemplify a stage in a report. He or she then has to answer questions which require both global and detailed understanding. There are two main types of question:
1 Target (to be answered while reading and providing a purpose for reading).
2 Comprehension (after reading).
The latter type range from questions seeking information to much more interpretive questions.

### 2 Tasks

This section looks at various aspects of the reading skills used in the previous section and applies them in a different context. The student is required to interpret and organise information in both textual and diagrammatic form. Often this involves transfer of information from text to diagram (a graph, chart, table, outline, etc.) or vice versa.

### 3 Language practice

Language concepts and structures (see Overview on p.5) which the student has been exposed to in the previous two sections are here explained and exploited. Most of the exercises are sentence based.

### 4 Writing

Finally the student is required to apply what he or she has learnt at both sentence and paragraph level. There is a variety of writing exercises including:
– model paragraphs;
– expansion of notes;
– completion of paragraphs;
– sequencing of sentences into paragraphs.

## Appendix

Like any appendix, this does not follow the organisation of the previous units but consists of supplementary tasks for practising writing personnel reports, memos and minutes. It also contains checklists for report writers.

## Key

It is important to point out to students that the answers given in the key may not always be the *only* correct versions, since writing of this type must allow students a certain amount of freedom. If they are unsure about the acceptability of an answer, they should refer to the teacher. Model answers are indicated by ▶M◀.

## Glossary

This contains difficult words from the report extracts with the page number of their first appearance and a simple explanation/paraphrase of the meaning in the context of the report.

## The units

Each unit provides approximately seven hours class or home study work, making a 50 hour course. Much of the work requires teacher monitoring rather than teacher instruction.

As the course deals with the task of report writing step by step, it is important that the students see the relationship between each stage. To clarify this, it may be useful to refer to the sections in the Appendix on 'Report organisation and structure' and 'Approaching the task' (pp.68–69).

### Reading and understanding

The students are given a role in the report reading activity. There is no reason why they shouldn't work in pairs or small groups reading and then discussing their answers to the questions, especially since many of the questions seek interpretive answers. They can then compare their answers with the key and ask the teacher for guidance where there is a discrepancy. Refer students to the glossary where necessary but encourage them to try and understand the meaning of new words from the context.

### Tasks

The tasks will promote discussion and again students working in pairs or small groups can approach the problems as a team.

### Language practice

The exercises in this section will need expanding to give further practice. For example, the students can be asked to find additional examples of use in the texts of the previous two sections.

### Writing

Note that the key for this section often only provides a model answer. Students whose main duty is report writing will certainly need more practice and the exercises in this section should provide a springboard for more extended report writing projects.

NB   For some exercises and tasks, a pocket calculator will be useful.

# STUDENT'S INTRODUCTION

This course is designed for:
1 Practising managers and secretarial personnel in fields such as administration, export, finance, general business, marketing, personnel and production.
2 Business studies students.
The level is intermediate to upper-intermediate.

## SELF-STUDY

The whole course can be followed on a self-study basis.

| | |
|---|---|
| *Introduction* | At the beginning of each unit, the purpose of the unit and its relationship to other units is explained (for an overall picture see the Appendix 'Approaching the task' p.69). |
| *Reading and understanding* | You will be given a role and asked one or two general questions. Read through the whole section to answer these. Read the section again and then answer the detailed questions which follow. Check your answers with the key. Use the glossary as little as possible. Try to understand new words from the context. |
| *Tasks* | These will force you to think more about the function of part of a report. Check your answers with the key after you have completed each task. |
| *Language practice* | In this section, you will be given practice in language you have seen in the previous two sections. Normally you will be given a model sentence (an example) on which to base your own sentences. |
| *Writing* | Now, you will practise writing paragraphs. Notice that there is often more than one correct version. The key only provides a model (▶M◀). |

# OVERVIEW

| | Reading and understanding | Tasks | Language practice | Writing |
|---|---|---|---|---|
| **Unit 1** Collecting the information | Assessing relevance, audience, fact and opinion | Distinguishing fact from opinion Precision Propositions and evidence | Comparing Reason and purpose Cause and effect | Terms of reference |
| **Unit 2** Using graphs and statistics | Assessing relevance, suitability Interpreting graphs | Transferring information from text to diagram | Amount and difference Quantity Graph description | Referencing illustrations Representing numbers |
| **Unit 3** Selecting and organising the material | Conciseness | Ordering Headings Classifying | Classification Active and passive Noun phrases | Writing notes Information sequence |
| **Unit 4** Presenting findings | Organisation Style | Ordering and reclassifying Personal and impersonal styles | Impersonal reporting Personal reporting Past perfect tense | Continuity and reference Paragraphing |
| **Unit 5** Concluding and recommending | Linking findings, conclusions and recommendations | Interpreting conclusions Matching recommendations | Degree Probability Recommendation | Conclusions Recommendations |
| **Unit 6** Summarising | Extracting main points Descriptive and evaluative summaries | Classifying information Simplifying | Contrast Condition Addition | Summaries |
| **Appendix** | A Routine writing tasks: Standard personnel reports Memos Minutes B Report organisation and structure: Standard pattern Approaching the task | | | |

# 1 COLLECTING THE INFORMATION

This first unit is about an important stage in writing an effective report – putting together the information. If you want to write a good report, you must be able to use the resources that are available and decide which information is useful and which is not.

## 1.1 READING AND UNDERSTANDING

In this section you will see four sets of information. You have to decide the importance of this information for the reporting task below.

Your company, Interbloc Inc., is a large manufacturer of industrial machinery. You work as Assistant Manager in the Supply Department of Interbloc's London headquarters. You have been asked by the Finance Manager to write the following report.

Terms of Reference:

1 To investigate the range of photocopying equipment on the market in order to make recommendations for the purchase of new machines for the HQ offices.
2 To establish the relative costs of renting, buying and leasing photocopying equipment and to make recommendations.

You have begun your investigation. So far, you have assembled four pieces of information. Read through these four pieces of evidence (A, B, C and D) and answer any questions that come before or after each one.

1 In deciding the relevance of some information, it is important to distinguish who it was written for. Was the following extract written for:
   a) photocopying equipment manufacturers?
   b) general readers?
   c) office supervisors?
   d) purchasers of photocopying equipment?

A ARTICLE FROM OFFICE EQUIPMENT SURVEY

It is essential to get the correct machine for the volume that is required. In order to do this, it is necessary to obtain accurate estimates of the number of copies you make. A large proportion of companies who have replied to the Office Equipment Survey have not made proper estimates. The result is that they are running the wrong machine or are below minimum billing.

We asked Charles Sands, a business equipment consultant, to suggest a simple method of checking copy costs. He told us, 'First, establish the monthly cost of your machine as £x. Over three years this is, say, 3.3% of capital cost. For example, a machine purchased for £2,670 gives a monthly cost of £88. Alternatively, work out a figure based on your own financial method. Because of high maintenance costs, a formula of £x + 1.25p per copy is required so as to cover most machines.

Taking a machine at £88 a month doing 7,000 copies, this works out at 2.5p per copy. Or, for 3,000, it equals 4.2p per copy. And then, of course, there's the paper, too.'

You should also be able to extract important details. Answer the following questions:
2  What is most important when buying a photocopier?
3  Why do many companies have the wrong machine?
4  How much is it necessary to allow per copy above the cost of the machine?
5  If the cost of a machine is £95 per month, what is the copy cost for 5,000 copies?

6  The second piece of evidence is the tapescript of an interview you had with Mrs Clarke, Office Supervisor in the Sales Department. During the interview, Mrs Clarke commented on the following aspects of the AX20 photocopier used in her office:
   a) speed
   b) situation
   c) breakdowns
   d) quality
   e) noise
While you are reading the tapescript, decide which of these factors is not relevant to your enquiry.

B  INTERVIEW WITH MRS CLARKE

I: Mrs Clarke, I'd like some information about the AX20 photocopier used here in this office. For example, its efficiency . . . suitability?
C: The worst thing, as far as I'm concerned, is its position. It's placed very close to my desk and it also blocks the filing cabinets. It's very difficult for people . . .
I: I see. How long does it take to do a copy?
C: I'm not sure exactly, but it's extremely slow. And there always seem to be a lot of people waiting to use it. And more important, it's always breaking down.
I: Can you be more specific on that last point?
C: I know the machine is unreliable because I had to call the engineer five times last month.
I: Yes, that's significant. What other disadvantages are there?
C: Well, I feel it's an extremely noisy machine . . . much noisier than the last one we had and the quality is not good either.
I: The quality?
C: Yes, according to my records, there were over 8% spoilt copies in June and nearly as many as that the month before . . .

When deciding on the relevance of information, it is important to judge the value of opinions. Answer the following questions:

7 In Mrs Clarke's opinion, what is the most disadvantageous thing about the photo-copier?

8 What evidence does Mrs Clarke give for poor quality?

9 What evidence does Mrs Clarke have for slow copy time?

10 Which of the following pieces of information would it be useful to obtain from Mrs Clarke:

   a) personnel permitted to use the photocopier?

   b) type of documents photocopied?

   c) number of photocopies done per day?

   d) type of copy paper used?

The next piece of evidence is much more factual.

C SUMMARY OF PREVIOUS REPORT MADE BY THE PURCHASING DEPARTMENT AT INTERBLOC HQ IN JULY 1978

---

The purpose of this report is to assess the relative costs of copy facilities based on different methods of payment. The methods examined are:

1 Rental  2 Leasing  3 Buying

1.1 The rate of rental depends on copy volume. On an AX20 at the minimum rate of 3,000 copies per month, the price is 2.9p per copy, excluding paper. At 10,000 copies a month, the rate is 1.75p. A total of £175.

2.1 On a five year lease, the monthly charge, depending on tax relief, is approximately £44.13. In addition, 1.1p per copy is required for maintenance and service. On 3,000 copies, this amounts to £77.13 a month. On 10,000, it is £154.13.

3.1 The capital cost of buying, after tax, is £1125.60. Over five years, that is £18.76 a month. Add running costs of 1.1p per copy and this gives a monthly total of £51.76 for 3,000 copies and £128.76 for 10,000.

---

11 When leasing, what does the machine charge depend on?

12 Which method gives the cheapest copy cost?

13 What is the copy cost at 3,000 copies per month when buying?

14 The fourth piece of evidence has been provided by Mr Madson of the Accounts Department at Interbloc. It is a written statement of his views. While you are reading the statement, decide if Mr Madson is:
   a) putting forward an argument against renting?
   b) putting forward an argument against buying?
   c) putting forward an argument for leasing?
   d) putting forward an argument for renting?

D  MR MADSON'S STATEMENT

The question of whether to lease, rent or buy is very complicated. It very much depends on the tax and cash position of a company. But one thing is clear; our present policy of buying is unwise. Because this type of equipment is constantly improving, it is necessary to make frequent changes. If you own a copier, you have to sell it. The trouble is that there is a very poor market for used machines. A secondary point is that Interbloc is a large company that does not need to build up its assets in this way or have a debt on the balance sheet. At the same time, the advantages of leasing have been overstated. Many companies have regarded leasing as a means of avoiding tax. In fact, it only postpones it. The company must face a tax bill in the end. The only way to avoid making payment is for the company to go on leasing at an increasing rate.

15 What is Mr Madson's principal argument against buying?
16 What have many companies misunderstood about leasing?
17 What causes companies to go on leasing at a higher level?
18 Now look back at the terms of reference on page 6. Which of the following would you like to know more about?
   a) costs of renting, buying and leasing equipment
   b) the range of photocopying equipment on the market

## 1.2  TASKS

In this section there are four passages from reports. In the first two (A and B), you must decide if some statements are facts or opinions.

### 1.2.1  Fact and opinion

When we prepare or read a report it is important to recognise what are facts and what are opinions. For example, Mrs Clarke, the Office Supervisor, told you:
*'I feel it's an extremely noisy copier.'*
This is clearly only Mrs Clarke's **opinion**. She gives no evidence in support of her statement. But she also said:
*'According to my records, there were 8% spoilt copies in June ...'*
This evidence is **fact**.
Such expressions as:
   in my view
   in my opinion
   it seems to me
tell us that the speaker is only giving an **opinion**.
Now read the following passage and complete the table after it.

A  ATTENDANCE AT TRAINING COURSES

> The company certainly has a problem with staff attendance at special training courses. This is particularly true for the supervisors' afternoon college courses. The college has reported as little as 30% attendance on some courses. I think there are a number of reasons for this situation. First of all, I have the feeling that the course is not made interesting or relevant for our staff. Secondly, the timing of the course on Friday afternoons is not suitable because the trainees are tired at the end of the week. A further point is the distance of the college from the factory. It is nearly one hour's journey. And finally, it is my view that many of the supervisors attending these courses are not suitable for them. The work is too hard for them.

| Information | Fact (✓) | Opinion (✓) |
|---|---|---|
| 1  Poor attendance at supervisors' course | | |
| 2  Course not interesting or relevant | | |
| 3  Course badly time-tabled | | |
| 4  College too far from the factory | | |
| 5  Supervisors not good enough for course | | |

Now read the following passage and complete the table below it.

B COMPANY SUGGESTION SCHEME

The present Suggestion Scheme at International Trucks has been a failure. This is evidenced by both the low number of suggestions made in 1982 (26) and the low number of successful suggestions (5). Above all, this failure is due, it seems to me, to the low state of staff morale at the moment. There are a number of other reasons. First, there are no guidelines for making suggestions which would make it easier for the staff. Second, the rewards for successful suggestions (£20–£100) have not increased for five years. Lastly, it is my view that the Suggestion Scheme Committee is not suitable and does not have the confidence of the staff.

| Information | Fact (✓) | Opinion (✓) |
|---|---|---|
| 1 Suggestion Scheme a failure | | |
| 2 Failure due to low state of staff morale | | |
| 3 Lack of guidelines | | |
| 4 Low rewards for successful suggestions | | |
| 5 Unsuitable committee | | |

## 1.2.2 Precise descriptions

It is important that we describe things exactly in a report. For example, '*The room's floor area is 120 square metres*' is a **precise** statement but '*The room is rather big*' only gives us an **opinion** about the size of the room.

Read the following passage and complete the table below it.

THE BERTA 6–41

The Berta 6-41 is a very economical photocopier with very low service requirements. We can safely say that it has the copying facilities of much larger machines. Yet it is compact, lightweight and extremely stylish. For example, it weighs only 22kg and its overall dimensions are 74 x 43 x 21 cm. There are no sheet handling problems with the machine because the paper is loaded in cassettes of 100 sheets. The time for the first copy is only 11.4 seconds. All in all, the Berta 6-41 is a reliable machine and good value for money.

| Statement on: | Precise (✓) | Imprecise (✓) |
|---|---|---|
| 1 Economy | | |
| 2 Service requirements | | |
| 3 Comparison with larger machines | | |
| 4 ...................... | | |
| 5 ...................... | | |
| 6 Handling | | |
| 7 ...................... | | |
| 8 Reliability and value | | |

## 1.2.3 Propositions and evidence

In the following passage a main proposition is presented. This proposition is supported by evidence. What the evidence is based on is also stated.

Read the passage and complete the table below it.

PRIVATE TELEPHONE CALLS

Management is concerned at the increasing use of company telephones for private calls by staff. There has been a large increase in the number of local calls made by staff, as registered during a recent check. Secondly, there has been a 22% increase in company telephone bills this year (allowing for price rises). This increase in costs is not the result, as our recent survey has shown, of i) business growth or ii) changes in business communication. Finally, many customers have complained that our lines are frequently busy. Staff are reminded that there are public pay phones in the building for private calls.

| *Proposition* | Increasing number of private calls | | |
|---|---|---|---|
| *Evidence* | a) ........................ ........................ | b) ........................ ........................ | lines busy |
| *Based on* | check | telephone bills | c) ........................ ........................ |

# 1.3  LANGUAGE PRACTICE

## 1.3.1  Comparing

Study the table below in which three photocopiers are presented.

| *Specifications* | | *Zenton 403* | *Arrow 2C* | *Berta 6-41* |
|---|---|---|---|---|
| 1  *Price* | *(£)* | *1,595* | *1,816* | *1,600* |
| 2  *First copy time* | *(secs)* | *8.4* | *9.0* | *11.4* |
| 3  *Output* | *(no/hour)* | *600* | *750* | *500* |
| 4  *Weight* | *(kg)* | *38* | *34* | *22* |
| 5  *Width* | *(cm)* | *70* | *68* | *74* |
| 6  *Reliability* | *(\*)* | ** | * | *** |

Notice how we can make statements about:

Price:   The Berta copier is *more expensive than* the Zenton, but *less expensive than* the Arrow. The Arrow is *the most expensive* and the Zenton is *the least expensive*.

First copy time:   The Arrow is *faster* than the Berta, but *slower* than the Zenton. The Zenton is *the fastest* and the Berta is *the slowest*.

Choose from the following adjectives to make sentences for 3–6:

high, reliable, heavy, deep, low, wide, narrow, light.

Remember, adjectives of more than two syllables, such as expensive, always use *more/less ... than* and *the most/least ...* .

## 1.3.2  Reason and purpose

We can express our reasons by using expressions such as *because of, owing to* and *due to*. For example:

┌────────────RESULT────────────┐     ┌────REASON────┐
The failure of the Suggestion Scheme is **due to** the low level of reward.

We can express purpose by using expressions such as *in order to* and *so as to*.

┌──────────SITUATION──────────┐     ┌──────────PURPOSE──────────┐
The company continued leasing **in order to** avoid making tax payments.

Use the following to make 8 sentences, linking each of the statements with one of those on the right.

| Result/Situation | → | Reason/Purpose |
|---|---|---|
| 1  A report was made<br>2  The training centre was established<br>3  The report was a failure<br>4  The training course was cancelled<br>5  Output went down<br>6  The photocopier was inefficient<br>7  They leased the machine<br>8  Efficiency was increased | in order to<br>because of | postpone tax payments<br>difficult trading conditions<br>assess the relative costs of photocopiers<br>poor maintenance facilities<br>imprecise terms of reference<br>low staff attendance<br>the low level of supervisory knowledge<br>improved training methods |

## 1.3.3  Cause and effect

Notice how we can link pairs of sentences to show cause and effect.

┌────── CAUSE ──────┐               ┌──EFFECT──┐
Ineffective management               Poor profits

Management was ineffective which **resulted in** / **caused** poor profits.

┌─EFFECT─┐               ┌────── CAUSE ──────┐
Poor profits               Ineffective management

Poor profits **resulted from** / **were caused by** ineffective management.

Now link the following ideas in a similar way:

| | |
|---|---|
| 1  Imprecise terms of reference | unsatisfactory report |
| 2  Low demand | expensive product |
| 3  The high level of leasing | higher level of taxation |
| 4  Lack of interest in the Suggestion Scheme | low staff morale |
| 5  The success of the report | careful planning |
| 6  The unsuitable photocopy service | poor maintenance of equipment |

# 1.4 WRITING

In this section you will be given practice in writing the first stage of a report – the terms of reference.

## 1.4.1 Terms of reference

Study the following table.

| Subject | Purpose |
|---|---|
| 1 Photocopying equipment on market | Recommend new machines for HQ offices |
| 2 Supervisors' training course | Recommend new methods of training |
| 3 Relative costs of renting, buying and leasing photocopiers | Establish most efficient method |
| 4 Company Suggestion Scheme | Identify problems with present scheme and recommend new scheme |
| 5 Staff use of company telephones for private calls | Assess the scale of this practice |
| 6 Management trainees' introductory course | Determine the reasons for high failure rates and recommend improvements |

Notice how we can use this table to write out terms of reference, e.g. sentence 1:
*The purpose of this report is to investigate the photocopying equipment on the market in order to recommend new machines for all the HQ offices.*
Write similar sentences for 2–6. Remember that expressions such as *in order to* and *so as to* will help you.

# 2 USING GRAPHS AND STATISTICS

This unit deals with the use of illustrations (graphs, tables and charts) in a report. Illustrations can be used to make a point in the text of the report. They must always be clear, simple and relevant to the objectives of the report.

## 2.1 READING AND UNDERSTANDING

In this section, you will see a range of illustrations. You have to decide on the relevance of these illustrations to the reporting task outlined as follows:
You work for a team of management consultants. You have been asked by your client, National Telecom, to prepare a report on productivity in the telecommunications industry. Here are your terms of reference:

> 1 To make international comparisons in order to assess factors influencing levels of productivity.
>
> 2 To compare up-to-date information on productivity in different telecom sectors with levels of telephone traffic.
>
> 3 To assess methods of measuring productivity with a view to recommending the most effective method.

1 Look at the two graphs that follow. Which of these sentences about them are true?
   a) There is a direct relation between telephone density and GNP.
   b) The higher the GNP, the higher the telephone density.
   c) GNP forecasts are a reliable way of predicting increases in telephone density.
   d) GNP is the only factor affecting telephone density.

A INTERNATIONAL COMPARISONS

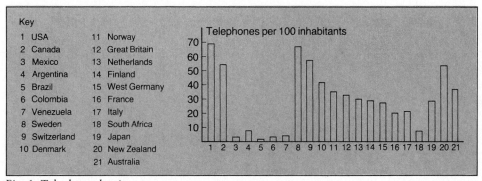

Fig. 1 Telephone density

15

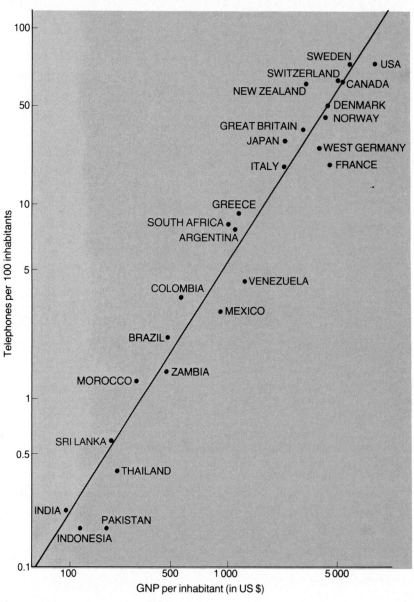

*Fig. 2*

Now answer the following detailed questions about the graphs.
2  On what basis are the countries arranged in fig. 1?
3  In fig. 2, the horizontal axis represents GNP/inhabitant. What does the vertical axis represent?
4  What does the solid line represent in fig. 2?

Now look at the following graph in which telephone density (telephones per 100 inhabitants) is plotted against telephone productivity (telephones per member of telephone company staff).

5 Which of the following statements are true?
   a) Telephone density in Morlanda is lower than in Sweden and the USA.
   b) Telephone productivity is lower in Morlanda than in Sweden and the USA.
   c) The forecast shows that density and productivity in Morlanda will catch up with Sweden and the USA.
   d) There is a direct relationship between productivity and density.
   e) Telephone density is the only factor affecting productivity.

B  TELEPHONE DENSITY AND PRODUCTIVITY

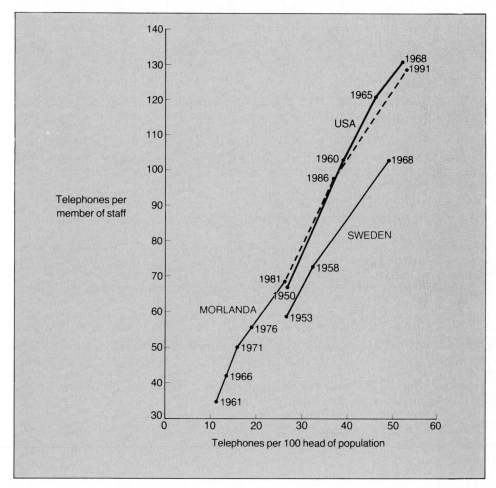

*Fig. 3*

Now answer these detailed questions:
6 What is the earliest year represented on the graph?
7 What is the most recent year for which actual figures are given?
8 What does the broken line represent?

17

The following table shows how productivity in National Telecom developed in the period 1968–1980.
9  Which of the following interpretations are correct?
   a)  As overall business productivity increased, telephone density also increased.
   b)  As manpower productivity increased, telephone density increased.
   c)  Engineering manpower productivity increased at the same rate as total telecom manpower productivity.

C  PERCENTAGE CHANGE PER ANNUM

|  |  | 1968-9 to 1973-4 | 1973-4 to 1978-9 | 1979-80 |
|---|---|---|---|---|
|  | **Outputs** |  |  |  |
| 1 | Revenue (at constant tariff) | 8.4 | 10.3 | 9.6 |
| 2 | Total stations | 4.6 | 6.6 | 8.1 |
| 3 | Total connections | 4.0 | 7.0 | 8.7 |
| 4 | Local calls | 6.6 | 7.8 | 11.6 |
| 5 | Trunk calls | 12.6 | 14.0 | 11.4 |
| 6 | Engineering work | 5.2 | 8.8 | 8.3 |
|  | **Inputs** |  |  |  |
| 7 | Expenditure (at constant prices) | 5.6 | 6.4 | 6.7 |
| 8 | Telecommunications manpower | 2.6 | 3.6 | 0.8 |
| 9 | Engineering manpower | 4.0 | 2.0 | 1.4 |
|  | **Productivity** |  |  |  |
| $1 \div 7$ | Overall (revenue/expenditure) | 2.6 | 3.6 | 2.7 |
| $1 \div 8$ | Telecommunications manpower | 5.7 | 7.8 | 10.0 |
| $6 \div 9$ | Engineering manpower | 1.1 | 6.2 | 6.7 |

*Table 1*

Now answer the following questions:
10  What type of telephone call increased most during the period 1968–1980?
11  How is the overall business productivity calculated?
12  How is telecom manpower productivity calculated?
13  How is engineering manpower productivity calculated?
14  Now look back at the terms of reference on page 15. Which of the terms of reference do the figures illustrate?
   a)  Fig. 1.
   b)  Fig. 2.
   c)  Fig. 3.
   d)  Table 1.
15  Which of the illustrations would you change to a different format (table – graph, graph – table) in order to make the points more clearly?

## 2.2 TASKS

In this section, you must interpret text and illustration by transferring information from text to illustration and from one type of illustration to another.

### 2.2.1

Read the following text and transfer the information in it to the graph that follows.

EXTRACT FROM MINUTES OF PRODUCTION MEETING, APRIL 1981

> Mr Dodds, Production Manager, reviewed 1980. He stated that demand exceeded supply for most of the year. In January, mainly because of the Christmas break, production fell below target by 150 units. This meant that the early part of February was spent in clearing the backlog of orders. To do this, the factory worked at full capacity for the whole month and reached a total of 890 units. It dropped slightly in the following two months (by 40 units) and levelled off at around 830 in May and June. July was our busiest month. Production peaked at 980 units before dropping to 80 units below the annual average in August. Once the summer holiday period ended, production climbed gradually to reach 800 again in September and it actually met our target in October. The last two months of the year were dogged by maintenance problems and by an industrial dispute at the end of November. The figure for November was well below average at 670 and December was only slightly better at 690.

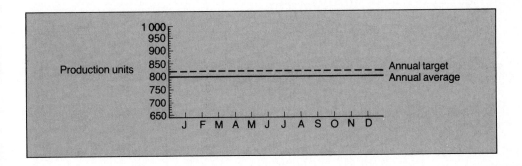

### 2.2.2

Transfer the information in this table to the line graph that follows it.

PERCENTAGE INCREASE/DECREASE IN COMPANY TRAINING AND PROFIT 1978–1983

| Year | 78 | 79 | 80 | 81 | 82 | 83 |
|---|---|---|---|---|---|---|
| Profit | +5.5 | +3.4 | +6.8 | +4.5 | −1.2 | +6.8 |
| Technical training | +2.0 | +1.6 | +0.7 | −0.3 | −1.3 | +0.8 |
| Management training | +3.0 | +2.2 | +3.1 | +2.9 | +1.6 | +4.0 |

Use the following lines when you transfer the information:
_ _ _ _ _ _ _ profit _____ technical training _ _ _ . _ _ . _ _ _ management training

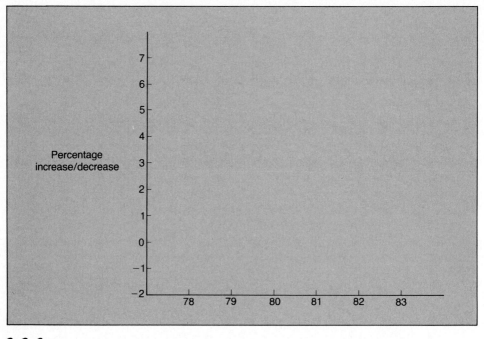

## 2.2.3

Decide which of the two illustrations best represents the following text.

WASHBRIGHT LTD SALES REPORT (EXTRACT)

The sales force has grown rapidly during the last five years. At
the same time, in-service training has been maintained for our
more senior sales staff. The results of our policies can be seen in
the marked increase in market share which our products have
gained:

Detergents  Up by 3% to a total market share of 23%. Of particular
note is the fact that our new product, 'Biowash',
captured 10% of the market by itself.

Soaps        Up by 2% to a total market share of 15%, with 'Savlux'
capturing 3% of the market.

Toothpaste  Up by 4% to a market share of 28%, with 'Fillfree'
capturing 4% of the market.

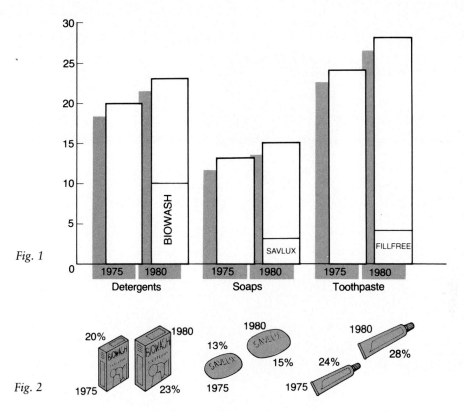

Fig. 1

Fig. 2

## 2.2.4

Transfer the information in this text to the pie chart that follows.

COMPANY TRAINING EXPENDITURE

In 1981, spending on training will increase in most sections of
the company although, as the figures make clear, the amounts for
Product and Line management will not be as high as in 1980. The
former will have £33,000 allocated, the latter £22,000. Personnel
in the Marketing and Research and Development departments were
often unable to take part in in-service training in 1980 because
of unusually heavy workloads. To compensate for this, we plan to
make large increases in their training budgets for 1981. £20,000
and £25,000 will be spent on Marketing and R & D respectively.
Finally, supervisory staff will have the same amount allocated as
this year. Total expenditure will be increased by £8,000.

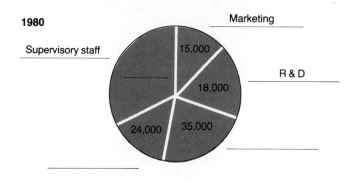

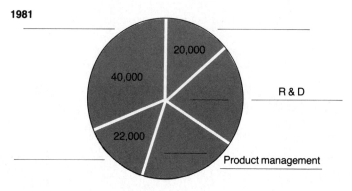

## 2.3  LANGUAGE PRACTICE

In this section you will practise language that is useful in statistical writing.

### 2.3.1  Amount and difference

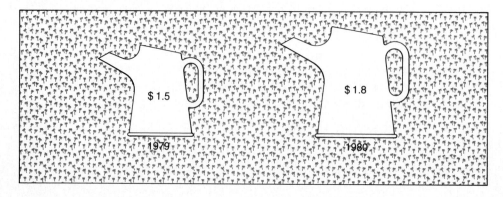

In 1979, the price of oil stood *at* $1.5.
Oil prices rose *by* $0.3 in 1980.
Oil prices rose *from* $1.5 *to* $1.8 in 1980.
There was an increase *of* $0.3 in 1980.

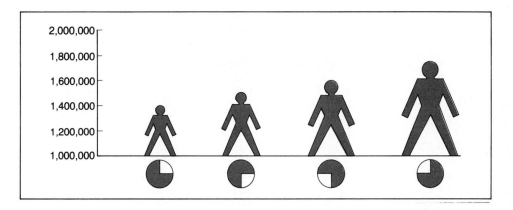

At the beginning of the year, unemployment stood *at* 1,400,000.
Unemployment rose *by* 350,000.
Unemployment rose *from* 1,400,000 *to* 1,750,000 during the year.
There was an increase *of* 350,000.

Now look at this graph showing sales and complete the sentences that follow.

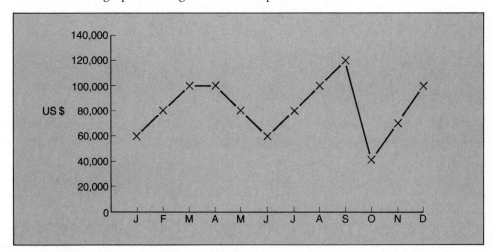

1  In February, sales increased ......... $80,000.
2  The following month, there was a further increase ......... $20,000.
3  In April, they remained constant ......... $100,000.
4  In the next two months, they dropped ......... $40,000.
5  As a result of this fall, they were back ......... $60,000 in June.
6  The next three months saw a steady rise ......... $120,000 in September.
7  This was followed by a dramatic fall ......... $40,000 in October.
8  Sales rose in December to finish the year ......... $100,000.

23

## 2.3.2 Quantity

|  | Countable (units) |  | Not countable (mass) |
|---|---|---|---|
| many<br>few | barrels<br>reports<br>machines<br>typewriters<br>desks<br>employees | much<br>little | oil<br>information<br>machinery<br>office equipment<br>furniture<br>manpower |

| Situation | → | Explanation |
|---|---|---|
| The price of oil is low | because<br>since | too much   oil is being produced. |
| Salaries are high | as | too few   qualified employees are available. |

Link the following situations and explanations in the same way.
1  The typists are overworked ................................ reports are being written.
2  Capacity is limited ................................ machinery is being repaired.
3  The employees are worried ................................ information has been given.
4  We must increase investment ................................ money has been spent.
5  Railway fares are rising ................................ passengers are using trains.
6  There is no need for overtime ................................ orders have been received recently.

## 2.3.3  Graph description

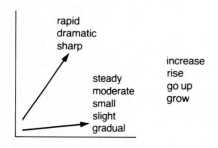

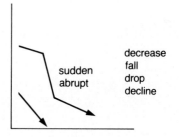

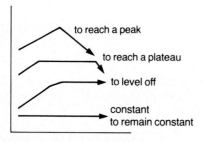

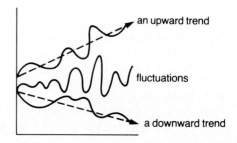

Use the information in this graph to complete the sentences that follow:

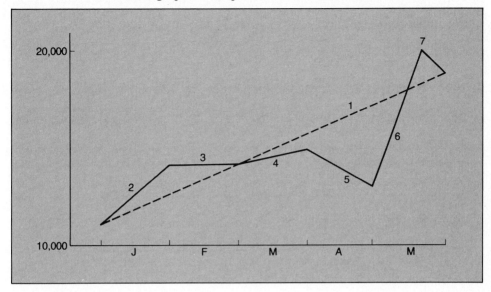

1  As the graph shows, there was an ...................................... in sales.
2  In January, sales ......................................... .
3  In February, sales ..........................................
4  before they ......................................... again ......................................... .
5  There was a ......................................... in April
6  then a ......................................... to
7  a ......................................... of 20,000 in May.

## 2.4  WRITING

In this section, you will practise:
– writing short paragraphs related to certain illustrations;
– writing numbers in full.

### 2.4.1  Referencing illustrations

Remember to be clear about referencing the illustrations in the text of the report. Note the following expressions:

*As is shown* | *in Fig. 1*        *The first column/row*
*As can be seen* | *in Table 2*        *Of particular note*
*(See Fig. 3)*        *NB (nota bene = note well)*
*The figure* | *above/below*
| *on the left/right*

Now complete the text related to the following table:

|  | 1977 | 1978 | 1979 | 1980 | 1981 | 1982 | 1983 |
|---|---|---|---|---|---|---|---|
| *Chemical* | 100 | 105 | 106 | 108 | 105 | 109 | 112 |
| *Sales* | 100 | 108 | 109 | 111 | 111 | 113 | 121 |
| *Operators* | 100 | 106 | 109 | 115 | 113 | 115 | 117 |
| *Engineers* | 100 | 108 | 109 | 109 | 103 | 110 | 114 |

The table ..................................... illustrates developments in productivity during the period 1977–1983. ....................................., the first ......................................, for the year 1977, represents a base year. The four ......................................, one for each department, demonstrate that productivity has risen steadily throughout the company, except for a slight drop in 1981 when there was an unusually high wage increase. ...................................... is the marked improvement for our sales force from 82 to 83.

## *2.4.2  Representing numbers*

Note the following points:

For numbers below ten, words are preferable to numerals:
**Not** *There were 5 files missing from the cabinet.*
**Use** *There were five files missing from the cabinet.*

Use numerals for page numbers, dates, figures, addresses and with %:
**Not** *-One-, Twenty-third July, fig. six, Four New Street, six%.*
**Use** *-1-, 23 July, fig. 6, 4 New Street, 6%.*

Do not use numerals for ordinate numbers:
**Not** *This is the 2nd report on the subject in 6 months.*
**Use** *This is the second report on the subject in six months.*

Do not use two numerals in succession:
**Not** *12 10 man teams.*
**Use** *Twelve ten-man teams.*

Do not use numerals at the beginning of a sentence:
**Not** *15 people were injured in the accident.*
**Use** *Fifteen people were injured in the accident.*

Do not use numerals for round number estimates:
**Not** *Roughly 200 employees were made redundant.*
**Use** *Roughly two hundred employees were made redundant.*

Correct the following paragraph:

---

Absenteeism has reached its highest level for 6 years. 3 years ago we had an average absentee level of four per cent. Despite our proposals, laid down in the 2nd 5-year productivity plan, absenteeism has risen to around three hundred workdays lost per year.
A distressing feature of absenteeism here is that only about 100 of the workdays lost were officially reported, i.e. the absentee telephoned or sent a doctor's note. The other sixty-five per cent gave no reasons for their absence.
We recommend that a new clause be added to the Contract of Employment, Para. two, page three:
'Employees who are absent without leave will have their earnings reduced by an amount equivalent to the number of hours lost.'

---

# 3 SELECTING AND ORGANISING THE MATERIAL

This unit deals with the selection and organisation of material for the final report. When the writer has assembled all the relevant material, he or she should be able to form some opinions. It is then necessary to decide how much information is needed in the report to support these opinions. Too much information will hide the point, too little information will not convince the reader.

## 3.1 READING AND UNDERSTANDING

You have been asked by your Personnel Director to review your company's existing recruitment procedure. This is shown in fig. 1.

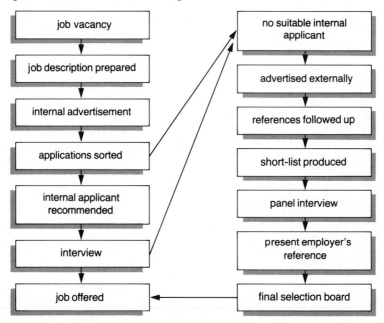

Fig. 1 Recruitment procedure

Terms of reference: to assess the recruitment procedure with a view to shortening the process and thus cutting costs. You have assembled all the information you need about the procedure and have come to the following conclusions:
– External advertising should only be carried out by job agencies.
– References should only be taken up on short-listed candidates.
– Panel interviews should only take place at the final selection stage.

Now read through draft report A and, keeping in mind the three conclusions above, decide if it says:

| | | |
|---|---|---|
| a) nothing<br>b) too little<br>c) the right amount<br>d) too much | about | 1 trade journals<br>2 job descriptions<br>3 length of interview<br>4 follow-up references<br>5 duration of procedure |

DRAFT REPORT A

| | |
|---|---|
| Job Vacancy | There have been 20 job vacancies during the last year, of which 15 have been due to retirement and five to new posts. |
| Job Description | For the five new posts, the relevant departments were asked to produce full job descriptions. In each case, this delayed advertising by two to three weeks. |
| Internal Advertising | Fifteen of the posts produced internal applications. For five of these, the internal candidates were rejected immediately and the procedure passed to external applications. Of the other ten, five more were rejected on the advice of their departments. Of the remaining five, only two were offered the post and just one accepted. |
| External Advertising | A total of 19 posts were eventually advertised externally. These advertisements were placed in national and trade journals as well as through job agencies.<br>An average of 80 applications were received for each post advertised in this way. On average, 60 applications came from national newspaper advertising, 10 from trade journals and 10 from job agencies. Of the eventual successful candidates, 16 resulted from job agency advertising. |
| Reference Follow-up | An average of 50% of applications were followed up by requesting references. On the basis of these, short-lists of between 10 and 15 were produced. |
| Panel Interview | The short-listed candidates were interviewed by a panel of three managers which included the Personnel Manager, a Departmental Director and the immediate superior. |
| Present Employer's Reference | An average of three present employers were contacted at this stage for each vacancy. |
| Final Selection Board | Posts were offered to the 20 first-choice candidates and accepted by 19 of them. In the one other case, the reserve (second choice) candidate was offered and accepted the post. |

What do the following refer to?
Example: ... of *which* ... (line 2). Answer: 'which' refers to the '20 job vacancies'.

6  In *each case*, ...         (l.6)       10  *These advertisements* ... (l.17)
7  ... *this* delayed ...      (l.6)       11  ... in *this way*.          (l.21)
8  ... five of *these* ...     (l.9)       12  ... at *this stage* ...     (l.36)
9  ... of the *other ten* ... (l.12)       13  ... the *one other case* ... (l.39)

Now read through draft report B and, still keeping in mind the three conclusions, decide if it says:

a) nothing
b) too little          about
c) the right amount
d) too much

14  trade journals
15  job descriptions
16  length of interview
17  follow-up of references
18  duration of procedure

DRAFT REPORT B

| Number of vacancies | Filled internally | Filled externally |
|---|---|---|
| 20 | 1 | 19 |

Table 1 Internal v. External Recruitment

| National Journals | | Trade Journals | | Job Agencies | |
|---|---|---|---|---|---|
| Applications received | Successful candidates | Applications received | Successful candidates | Applications received | Successful candidates |
| 1140 | 2 | 190 | 1 | 194 | 16 |

Table 2 Methods of External Advertising

As can be seen from Table 1 above, external advertising has been much more effective than internal advertising. In addition, Table 2 clearly shows that the job agencies are our most effective method of external recruitment.

An average of 85 man hours was spent on recruitment for each post. 40% of this time was spent on sorting applications, 30% on following up and responding to references, 20% on interviewing and 10% at the final selection board stage.

## 3.2 TASKS

### 3.2.1

Selection of material will be easier if the information you have assembled is well-organised. Read the following, badly-organised, text and then complete the task.

PROMOTION PROCEDURES

All managers should have a promotion review every two years. This does not mean that promotion cannot take place in the interim. However, promotion is normally gained after the promotion review session.

The procedure for conducting a promotion review is that the promotion review panel meets after having received SOPs (Standards of Performance) from all departments. Before asking the employee in for an informal interview, the review panel meet and discuss each employee. The panel should analyse not only the employee's past record but also his or her potential in the future. This will mean that the panel must have previously obtained up-to-date information on promotion possibilities. When they have done all this, they can invite the employee to an informal interview.

The informal interview should aim to assess the employee's own expectations and ambitions. Having completed this session, the panel should meet privately to decide on recommendations which are finally submitted to the Board.

These six stages are in the wrong order. Put the identifying letter for each stage in one of the boxes so that they are in the correct order:

a) review panel second meeting  d) recommendations to Board
b) informal interview  e) receive promotion possibility update
c) review panel first meeting  f) receive SOPs

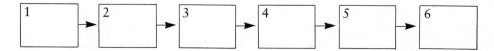

## 3.2.2

Selection and organisation will also be simpler if paragraphs have suitable headings. Look at the paragraphs from this report and decide which of the headings after the report they best come under.

REPORT ON PROJECT 551B IN ZIMBABWE

a) Contracts were binding under both British and local law. In particular, terms for breach of contract were given in both currencies.
b) All personnel going to work overseas had a full medical check-up. Inoculations, where necessary, were given well in advance of departure.
c) All accounts were submitted at the end of each month. They were processed in the normal way.
d) Travel back to the UK was paid for by the company once a year. In addition, 50% of fares were paid in special cases in which there was ill health or a death in the family.
e) All disputes concerning personnel were settled in the country of operation.

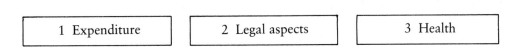

| 1 Expenditure | 2 Legal aspects | 3 Health |

## 3.2.3

It will also be easier to select material if the assembled information is well classified. Read this text and complete the organigram that follows.

REORGANISATION OF PERSONNEL DEPARTMENT

The Personnel Department was reorganised at the beginning of the year. Lines of communication and responsibilities were clarified under the new structure.

The Personnel Director kept overall responsibility for the department. However, instead of two large sections under him, Administration and Planning, there were, in the new structure, four sections: Recruitment, Training, Payments and Career Development. Each of these sections contains both administrative and planning functions.

The first section, Recruitment, has a staff of 10, headed by the Recruitment Manager. Besides internal and external recruitment, their responsibilities include the writing of job descriptions and a share of the manpower planning.

This latter responsibility is also the concern of the Training section. It has a staff of five, including the Training Manager. They are responsible for both in-house and external training at all levels within the company, from management training for senior staff down to technical courses for the Works Department.

The Payments section has a largely administrative role but is also involved in planning and implementing new salary structures and bonus schemes. The work of its staff of seven consists mainly, however, of administering the payment of wages, salaries and pensions to present and former employees.

Lastly, Career Development deals with employees' career development from recruitment to retirement. They have two staff who are responsible for updating computerised personnel records and another two who work closely with the Training section on manpower planning. They are headed by the Manpower Planning Manager.

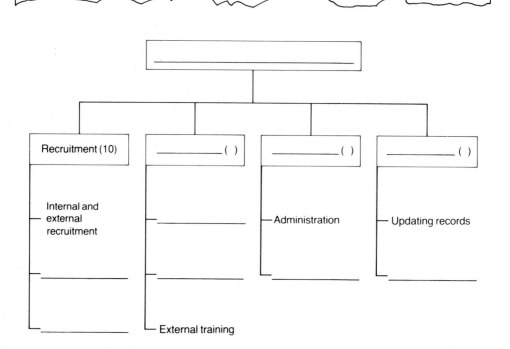

# 3.3  LANGUAGE PRACTICE

## 3.3.1  Classification

Main and sub parts

... is made up of ...       ... can be/is broken down into ...
... consists of ...          ... can be/is divided into ...
... includes ...             ... can be/is separated into ...

Hierarchical structure

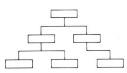

above/below          over/under
on the same level    at the top
headed by            at the bottom

Additional parts

besides ... ,        in addition to ...
not only ... but     ...also...
also ...

Examples:  The Personnel Department *is divided into* five sections.
One section, Training, *consists of* five staff.
The Division *is headed by* an Executive Director. *Below* him, there are three line managers.
There are six other directors on the Board *in addition* to the Managing Director.

Use the organigram to help you complete the following sentences:

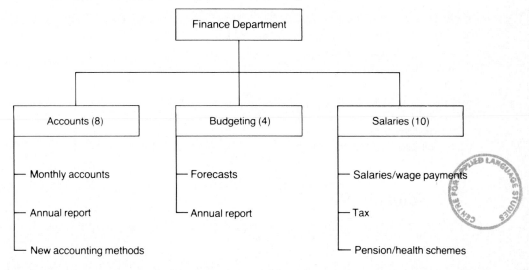

1  The Finance Department ......................... by the Finance Director.
2  It ......................... three sections.
3  ......................... the monthly accounts, the Accounts section shares responsibility for the annual report.
4  The Budgeting section ......................... four members of staff.
5  They are responsible ......................... for forecasts ......................... for the annual report.
6  The Salaries section, which ......................... 10 staff, deals with salary and wage payments.
7  ......................... these payments, it ......................... has responsibility for tax and pension and health schemes.

## 3.3.2  Active and passive

USE   Compare these two sentences:
Active: *The Promotion Review Panel* meets and discusses each candidate.
Passive: *Each candidate* is met and discussed (by the Promotion Review Panel).
Notice how the passive is used to emphasise the candidate instead of the Promotion Review Panel.
FORMATION   Active: ... *meets* and *discusses* ...
                    Passive: ... *is met* and (is) *discussed* ...

Now put the verbs in the following description in the active or the passive.

```
The Information Services Department ............
(divide) into two sections. The first, Statistical
Data, ............ (provide) information from a
data bank for all other departments. The second,
Support Services, ............ (deal) with
requests for specific information. When a request
............ (receive), one member of the team
............ (allocate) to the task and then
............ (carry out) all the necessary
research.
The department ............ (staff) by five
information officers who ............ (work) as a
team. A team leader ............ (appoint) for a
six month period. He or she is responsible for
allocating tasks within the group. The position of
team leader ............ (rotate) so that each
member of the group ............ (act) as leader
at some stage.
```

## 3.3.3  Noun phrases

Reports are often formalised by using noun phrases.
Example: We propose *to advertise externally.*
            *External advertising* is proposed.

34

Make noun phrases for the following sentences in a similar way:

1  We recommend that employees retire at the age of 65.
   A ..................... of 65 is recommended.
2  We need a manager responsible for developing careers.
   A ..................... is needed.
3  We suggest that posts are advertised by job agencies.
   ..................... is suggested.
4  We would prefer to train staff internally.
   ..................... would be preferred.
5  We should cost advertising in national newspapers.
   ..................... should be costed.
6  We must request senior management to make recommendations.
   ..................... must be requested.
7  We recommend that material is collected carefully.
   ..................... is recommended.
8  We advise you to select the material well.
   ..................... is advised.


## 3.4  WRITING


### 3.4.1  Writing notes

Read this paragraph and complete the outline:

> If the working week is shortened, there will be some immediate and
> some long-term effects. One of the immediate effects will be an
> increase in overtime worked. This will mean a rise in labour costs
> per production unit. One of the long-term effects will be a
> decrease in the flexibility of the work-force because employees
> will be more confined to their own work-places. Consequently,
> there will be a decrease in work experience and exchange.

Heading: .............................................................................................................

1  ............................. effects

   .................................. ➤ ..................................

2  ............................. effects

   .................................. ➤ .................................. ➤ .........................

   .........................

## 3.4.2 *Information sequence*

Use the following flow chart to help you complete the text that follows.

A COMPLAINTS PROCEDURE

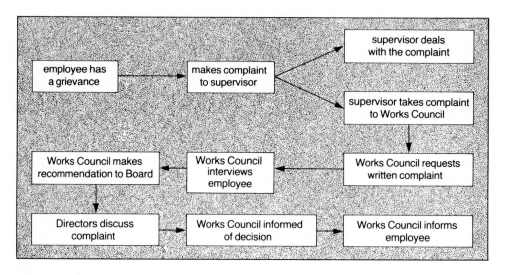

When a supervisor ........................................, he either ........................................,
or ........................................ . This body ........................................ before
........................................ the employee. Having discussed the complaint, the Works
Council ........................................ . Here they ........................................ and then
........................................ . Finally, the Works Council ........................................ .

Look at these **time sequence** markers:   First, ...
                                            Then ...
                                            When ...
                                            Before ...
                                            After ...
                                            Having ...
                                            Finally, ...

and at these **reference** words:   This/these
                                    They/he/she/it

Complete the following passage:

B NOTICE PROCEDURE

........ written notice is given, the supervisor passes ........ to the
Factory Manager. ........ will ........ ask the employee for an informal
chat about it ........ formally accepting ....... . ........ accepted
notice, the Factory Manager must inform the Personnel Department. ......
check their records and inform the employee how much holiday ........ is
due. ........ can take his holiday ........ or after the end of his
notice. ........, the employee must remember to return his work sheet
........ he leaves.

36

# 4 PRESENTING FINDINGS

The findings are the main part of the report. When the material has been selected and organised, you must present the findings as clearly as possible. You must decide whether a formal or informal style and personal or impersonal tone are appropriate.

## 4.1  READING AND UNDERSTANDING

As you read the following report, decide how much the findings meet the objectives of the introduction. Also decide whether the report is organised chronologically (according to time) or logically (according to a sequence of ideas).

---

CONFIDENTIAL REPORT ON FINANCE DIRECTOR S. HART

Introduction
This report aims to assess the performance of S. Hart, Finance Director, during the year 1981. In particular, it aims to review his actions and decisions in the following areas:
        a) General financial control
        b) Budgetary control
        c) Staff relations

Findings
S. Hart was appointed Financial Director in January 1981. He had previously been Chief Accountant in the company.
    For the first three months in his new position Mr Hart worked alongside Mr Gwent, his predecessor. At his first General Management Meeting, he was asked how he saw his role in the company. He replied that he thought his primary responsibility was to exert tight financial control particularly on 'running costs'.
    In April 1981, he submitted a first quarter financial report which already showed a slight decrease in current costs. At this meeting, the Marketing Director commented that the Spring advertising campaign had been delayed by the Finance Department's slowness in approving the expenditure.
    In June 1981, two junior members of the Finance Department resigned and went to work for one of our competitors.
    The second quarter financial report showed costs running considerably below forecast. The Marketing Director complained at the Management Meeting that his advertising budget had again been restricted. The problem was in getting funds from the Finance Department.
    In the following month, F. Flynn, the Finance Director's assistant, asked to be moved to another department. He said he could not work any longer with Mr Hart.
    In October, Mr Hart presented his 1982 budget. This was based on pessimistic forecasts for sales, and a planned 18% reduction in running costs and 5% reduction in fixed costs. The third quarter financial report had shown a marked drop in income matched by an even sharper drop in costs.
    In November 1981, the Marketing Director resigned saying: 'If he stays, I go.' It was understood that he was speaking about the Finance Director. Final figures for the year showed a good level of profitability (slightly higher than expected) but an alarming downward trend in sales.

---

1  What experience did Mr Hart have for this job?
2  For how long did Mr Hart work alone in 1981?
3  What did he consider his main duty?
4  In which area did he have most success?
5  How many staff left the department during the year?
6  Why did the Marketing Director leave?
7  In what other way could these findings be presented?
8  What style is the report written in:
   a)  formal or informal?   b)  personal or impersonal?

# 4.2 TASKS

## 4.2.1

Read the following chronological biodata and then reorganise them logically under the headings below.

| George Henry Moore | | | |
|---|---|---|---|
| | a ) | Date of birth | 13.5.53 |
| | b ) | Primary school | 58–64 |
| | c ) | Tonsilitis operation | 64 |
| | d ) | Junior Chess Champion | 64 |
| | e ) | Secondary school | 64–71 |
| | f ) | Trainee Engineer, AEB Ltd | 71–73 |
| | g ) | Polytechnic of North London | 73–76 |
| | h ) | Diploma in Electronics | 76 |
| | i ) | Electronics Engineer, AEB Ltd | 76–78 |
| | j ) | Married to Anna Maple | 77 |
| | k ) | London Business School | 78–79 |
| | l ) | Diploma in Business Studies | 79 |
| | m ) | 4 weeks in hospital after rock-climbing accident | 79 |
| | n ) | Birth of daughter, Emily Jane | 79 |
| | o ) | Sales Engineer, Telelec Ltd | 79–81 |
| | p ) | Senior Sales Engineer, Telelec Ltd | 81– |

Headings:  Personal details / Education / Qualifications / Work experience / Health / Hobbies

## 4.2.2

Read this tapescript of a finance meeting. Complete the two versions of the report that follow the tapescript.

| Mr Field: (Finance Director) | Interest rates are likely to fall. There's no way those guys in the States are going to keep them so high. |
|---|---|
| Mrs Powers: (Accounts Manager) | You may be right, but I doubt if they'll come down very soon. After all, American banks are never in a hurry about these things. |
| Mr Field: | Oh, I don't know. I reckon we could see a drop of 1 or even $1\frac{1}{2}\%$ early next week. |
| Mrs Powers: | Surely not. The most we can expect is $\frac{1}{2}\%$ and not for at least a month. I think . . . |
| Mr Keen: (Chairman) | We don't seem to be getting anywhere. Let's move on to the next point. |

EXTRACT FROM REPORT ON FINANCE MEETING: 19.12.82

INTEREST RATES

a) The short term future of ......................... was discussed. Opinions varied as to both ......................... and by ......................... interest rates would fall. It was suggested that they would fall by between ......................... and .........................% in ......................... week to ......................... month's time.

b) We discussed the probable drop in interest rates. ......................... believed that there would be a 1 to 1½% fall within the next week whereas ......................... thought there would be a maximum fall of ½% and not for at least one month.

What difference do you notice between two versions? Which of them do you prefer and why?

## 4.2.3 Style

Match the following extracts from reports with the styles listed on the right.

1 I think we should go ahead and invest in this project. If we don't, we'll be missing a golden opportunity.

    a) impersonal, formal and very sure

2 Investment in this project is imperative. Failure to invest would mean a missed opportunity.

    b) personal and unsure

3 No time should be wasted in advertising the post. Any delay will certainly result in less efficiency.

    c) impersonal and very sure

4 We should consider advertising the post. If we don't, it could lead to a reduction in efficiency.

    d) personal and informal

Now consider which of the following features are present in the above extracts:

|  | 1 | 2 | 3 | 4 |
|---|---|---|---|---|
| Personal pronouns | | | | |
| Passives | | | | |
| Idiomatic phrases | | | | |
| Expressions of certainty | | | | |
| Expressions of possibility | | | | |

## 4.3 LANGUAGE PRACTICE

## 4.3.1 Impersonal reporting

Here are some useful expressions for reporting meetings or discussions impersonally.

| *Topic/subject* | X was discussed. |
| | X was considered. |
| *Opinion* | It was felt that ... |
| | Opinions varied about ... |
| | Different opinions were expressed about ... |

| *Agreement/disagreement* | It was agreed that ... |
| | There was no agreement about ... |
| *Recommendation* | It was suggested that ... |
| | It was recommended that ... |
| | It was proposed that ... |
| *Conclusion* | It was concluded that ... |
| | No conclusions were reached about ... |
| | It was decided that ... |

Now report the following statements:

1  We've been talking for several hours about levels of investment.
2  Most of us think that we should increase our investment in the manufacturing sector.
3  We have heard a wide range of opinions on the subject of trade with China.
4  So we all agree that the advertising budget should be increased by 5%.
5  Mr Stevens has suggested that we double our spending on TV advertising.
6  I personally recommend that we leave it at the same level.
7  We don't seem to be able to reach agreement on the question of advertising.
8  I propose we postpone this matter until next week.
9  We all feel that we have spent enough time on this question.
10  We agreed with Peter when he said that we should allow more time for this question at the next meeting.

## 4.3.2   Personal reporting

Here are some guidelines for reporting meetings personally:

*Verb changes*    Present ——► Past
'I *think* the Financial Director should resign.'
——► He said he *thought* the Financial Director should resign.
Future 'will' ——► Conditional 'would'
'Prices *will level off* next year.'
——► She said that prices *would level off* next year.
Past ——► Past perfect
'Sales *reached* a peak in August last year.'
——► He reported that sales *had reached* a peak in ...

*Question changes*    Use of if/whether
'Do you think prices will increase?'
——► He asked us *if we thought* prices *would increase*.
——► He asked us *whether we thought* prices *would increase*.
Wh-words
'When do you expect sales to improve?'
——► He asked us *when we expected* sales to improve.

Now write a report based on this extract from the tapescript of the finance meeting:

```
Mr Field:     I feel the bank's lending policy must change. In the
              present economic climate we should be helping more
              small companies.

Mrs Powers:   I agree, but the problem is that small companies are
              often afraid to approach the banks for a loan.

Mr Field:     Do you think so? I met a local businessman recently
              who was trying to raise capital for investment in new
              machinery. He had tried the banks and found their
              terms very unfavourable.

Mrs Powers:   Yes, I'm sure that there are some small firms that
              would like to borrow from us but there are many others
              who won't come near us. Have you seen the latest
              borrowing figures?

Mr Field:     No, I haven't, but . . .

Mr Keen:      Well, it seems we should improve things in two ways.
              Firstly our image and secondly our actual lending
              terms.
```

## 4.3.3 *Past perfect tense*

There are two major uses: a) in reporting speech (see previous exercise)
b) in reporting the distant past

<--------- distant past <----------- past <------------- present
      *'previously'*                   *'March 1980'*                    *'now'*

►Mr Smith *was appointed* in March 1980. He *had previously been* our Chief Accountant.

Use this table to complete the sentences that follow.

| Subject | Distant past | Past |
|---|---|---|
| Mr Kent | Chairman of Atlas Holdings | retired in 1982 |
| Profits | £3.4m in 1968 | £2.5m in 1969 |
| Rationalisations | over-capacity in factory | introduced in 1970 |
| Company pension scheme | a good year in 1971 | started in 1972 |
| Costs | effects of oil crisis | stabilised last year |
| Interest rates | drop in 1977 | rose in 1978 |
| Fentons Ltd | drop in market share in early 70s | bankrupt in 1975 |
| New agreement | vote against strike | signed in 1979 |

1 Before Mr Kent ................. in 1982, he ................. (hold) the position of Chairman for six years.
2 Profits ................. £2.5m in 1969. The year before they ................. (reach) £3.4m.
3 Rationalisations ................. in 1970 to deal with the over-capacity which ................. (build up).
4 The company, having ................. (have) a good year in 1971, ................. (set up) a pension scheme in 1972.
5 After the company ................. (recover) from the effects of the oil crisis, costs ................. last year.

6 Before interest rates ................. in 1978, there ................. (be) a drop.
7 Prior to their bankruptcy in 75, Fentons Ltd ................. (lose) a lot of their market share in the early 70s.
8 A new agreement ................. in 1979 after the employees ................. (vote) against strike action.

# 4.4  WRITING

## 4.4.1   Continuity and reference

Organise the following sentences to compose two paragraphs under the heading below.
1 In particular, the Marketing Director complained frequently of difficulty in receiving funds for advertising campaigns.
2 Financial results during the year 1981 indicate Mr Hart's ability to reduce costs significantly.
3 There is evidence to suggest that Mr Hart's control over departmental budgets was also very rigid.
4 Furthermore, the Finance Director's budget forecasts for 1982 were considerably lower than other departmental budgets.
5 By the end of the year, they had dropped significantly below forecast levels.
6 This is evidenced by the downward trend in running costs throughout the year.

a) *General Financial Control*          b) *Budgetary Control*

Now look back at the confidential report in 4.1 (p.37) and extract relevant information under the heading (c) *Staff Relations*. Write this up as a paragraph.

## 4.4.2   Paragraphing

Here are some complete and some incomplete sentences in the wrong order. Reorder them so that they create two well-formed paragraphs, one for the whole group, the other for the UK.

... while the rest was due to external disputes ...
Non-European subsidiaries showed a rise to 16%.
In Europe, the German company's results were much better ...
... such as the transport strike in May.
... while severe problems were still faced by our companies in France and the UK.
Industrial disputes have contributed largely to the drop in operating profits in the UK.
Operating profits in the whole group have increased by 3% to an average of 7%.
Internal disputes accounted for £3m ...

# 5 CONCLUDING AND RECOMMENDING

This unit deals with two separate stages in a report, the conclusions and the recommendations. However these two stages are connected logically. Conclusions are drawn when the findings have been analysed. Recommendations are practical courses of action based on the conclusions.

## 5.1 READING AND UNDERSTANDING

You work for an agricultural machinery manufacturer, Ferton PLC. You have been asked to write a report with the following terms of reference: to investigate the reasons for a drop in Ferton tractor sales in Morlanda in order to recommend action to recapture market share.
Your investigation revealed the following sales statistics:

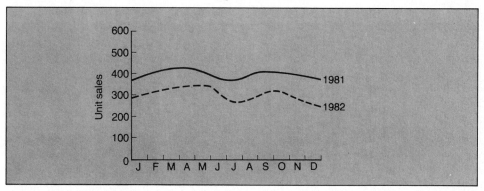

Your findings can be stated as follows:
a) The total volume of sales dropped.
b) There was a very significant drop in sales during the summer months.
c) The trend for the year was almost identical to the previous year.

Based on these findings and on the other evidence you conclude that the poor sales are due to the following factors:
a) The recent entry onto the market of a new competitor, JDC Tractors.
b) The main agent takes his holiday during the summer months.
c) The agent's deputy made few contacts during this period.
d) The usual seasonal influences.

1 What is the purpose of the investigation?
2 In which months did sales reach their peak?
3 In which month did sales have their low point?
4 Which of the following seasonal factors would explain the trend?
   a) Farmers generally buy tractors in the first three months of the year.
   b) Government subsidies to farmers are paid out in April.

   c) Farmers buy a lot of machinery during the summer harvest months.

   d) A lot of farmers replace their tractors after heavy use in harvest months.

   e) A lot of farmers buy tractors during the ploughing season (November and December).

5  Which of the following recommendations seem both logical and appropriate?

   a) to make a comparative study of Ferton and JDC Tractors

   b) to improve the product available in Morlanda

   c) to increase advertising during the summer months

   d) to replace the present agent

   e) to persuade the agent to take less holiday in the summer

   f) to discuss the work of the deputy agent with the main agent

   g) to increase promotion just before subsidies are paid out

   h) to pay the agent more commission

You are the Marketing Research Manager for JDC Tractors. You have been asked to report on the prospects for sales in Morlanda in 1983. Your terms of reference are:
– to forecast sales for the three tractors in the product range
– to assess the strength of established manufacturers
– to make necessary recommendations for the forecast to be realised
You have drawn up the following projections and, based on them, your recommendations:

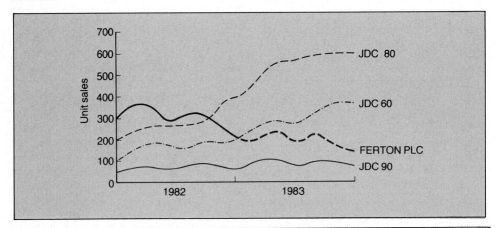

### Promotion

Promotion should concentrate on our middle range tractor (JDC 80) while stock levels of the top of the range product (JDC 90) could easily be reduced to lower levels. A more aggressive advertising campaign to stress the JDC product advantages over our main competitor, Ferton PLC, might be considered.

### Personnel

It is also recommended that agency contracts should not be renewed and that two salesmen be recruited for direct selling once the agency contracts have expired.

6  Why should promotion efforts concentrate on the JDC 80?
7  Why can JDC 90 stock levels be reduced?
8  Why do you think Ferton PLC sales are likely to continue falling?
9  Which of the following conclusions support the recommendations above?
   a) It is likely that the JDC 80 will continue to be the model in greatest demand.
   b) Sales of the JDC 60 are expected to rise gradually.
   c) Sales of the JDC 90 will remain constant in 1983.
   d) Our main competitor, Ferton PLC, relies on agents to sell its products.
   e) Our agents contributed less than 10% during 1982.
   f) Ferton's products will probably lose market share in 1983.

# 5.2  TASKS

## 5.2.1

Complete the key and graph by referring to the following conclusions taken from a sales report dated 12.3.82.

CONCLUSIONS

> – Sales of tennis equipment have been consistently higher in the summer months (July and August).
> – Our change in pricing policy for golf equipment led to a rapid increase in sales from the beginning of 1980.
> – Football equipment sales have continued to drop since the European Cup in the summer of 1980.
> – Squash equipment sales have risen gradually in line with the expansion of the market since 1980.

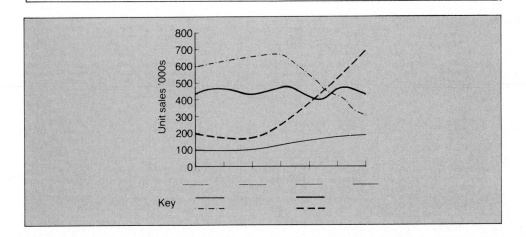

## 5.2.2

On the basis of the conclusions in 5.2.1, you have been asked to recommend appropriate action. Match up Action, Product and Purpose in the following table.

| *Action* | *Product* | *Purpose* |
|---|---|---|
| 1  Sponsorship of winter indoor championships | a)  golf equipment | w)  reverse downward trend |
| 2  Continue competitive pricing policy | b)  tennis equipment | x)  boost all-year-round sales |
| 3  Pre-European Cup sales campaign | c)  squash equipment | y)  prepare for gradual increased demand in expanding market |
| 4  Increase the number of distribution outlets | d)  football equipment | z)  maintain rate of sales increase |

## 5.2.3

Complete the findings in this report after reading the conclusions and recommendations it makes.

Findings

Record of F. Jones, junior salesman:

|  | F. Jones | Total (10 salesmen) |
|---|---|---|
| Repeat business | _____ | £1,400,000 |
| New clients | _____ | £550,000 |
| Lost clients | _____ | £220,000 |

Conclusions

Jones's performance last year was above average. He achieved 10% higher results than average with existing customers. His success in cold-contact selling is shown by the £75,000 worth of new business. However the loss of £33,000 of existing business indicates a major weakness in his after-sales strategy.

Recommendations

Jones should be sent on an after-sales training course at the earliest possible date.

## 5.2.4

Use this breakdown to complete the conclusions.

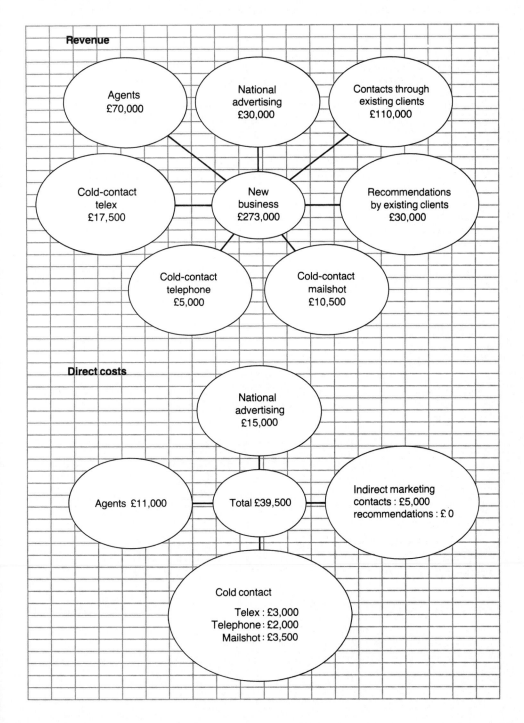

*Conclusions*

1 ............................ from new customers who know our existing clients accounts for more than half our new business.
2 As far as direct marketing is concerned, the work of ........................ is the most productive and cost-effective.
3 ........................ are relatively unsuccessful with an approximate 3:1 revenue/cost ratio.
4 In cold-contact marketing ........................ has given us the best return while ........................ is both our least productive and least cost-effective.

Which of the following recommendations are appropriate?

1 All efforts must be made to maintain good contacts with existing clients.
2 The appointment of a client relations manager might be considered in view of the large proportion of new business through existing clients.
3 Spending on national advertising should be increased.
4 A closer examination of the returns from national advertising is recommended.
5 The telephone should be our main channel for cold-contact selling.
6 We should concentrate on the use of telex for cold-contact selling.
7 A more integrated cold-contact selling strategy might be attempted.

# 5.3  LANGUAGE PRACTICE

## 5.3.1  Degree

We can modify statements about change by using adjectives or adverbs which indicate the degree of change:

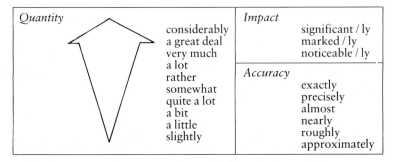

| Quantity | Impact |
|---|---|
| considerably | significant / ly |
| a great deal | marked / ly |
| very much | noticeable / ly |
| a lot | |
| rather | Accuracy |
| somewhat | exactly |
| quite a lot | precisely |
| a bit | almost |
| a little | nearly |
| slightly | roughly |
| | approximately |

Use the information in the following bar charts to complete the sentences:

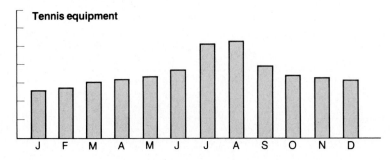

Tennis equipment

J  F  M  A  M  J  J  A  S  O  N  D

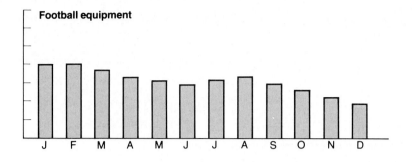

**Football equipment**

J F M A M J J A S O N D

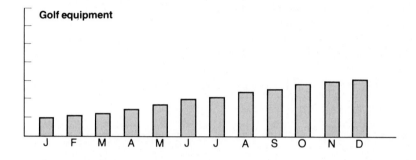

**Golf equipment**

J F M A M J J A S O N D

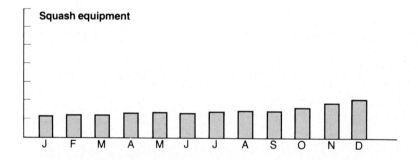

**Squash equipment**

J F M A M J J A S O N D

1  Sales of tennis equipment were ................. higher in July and August.
2  They were ................. lower in December than in November.
3  There was a ................. downward trend in football sales over the year.
4  December sales were ................. half our January sales.
5  In fact our December sales were ................. 33⅓% down on the June figure.
6  Golf equipment sales grew ................. in the first three months.
7  From April onwards, there was a ................. upward trend.
8  By December they were ................. treble the January figure.
9  Squash sales had a ................. slower rate of increase than golf sales.
10  However sales improved ................. over the last three months.

## 5.3.2 Probability

When forecasting we can indicate chances of reaching certain targets in the following way:

| | |
|---|---|
| *Certain* | ... will (definitely) reach ... |
| (100%) | ... are sure to reach ... |
| | ... are certain to reach ... |
| *Probable* | ... are likely to reach ... |
| (more than 60% certain) | ... will probably reach ... |
| | ... should reach ... |
| | ... are expected to reach ... |
| *Possible* | ... may reach ... |
| (more than 30% certain) | ... will possibly reach ... |
| | ... could reach ... |
| | ... might reach ... |
| *Improbable* | ... probably won't reach ... |
| (less than 30% certain) | ... are unlikely to reach ... |
| *Certain* | ... will (definitely) not reach ... |
| (0%) | ... are certain not to reach ... |

Use this bell curve to complete the sentences that follow:

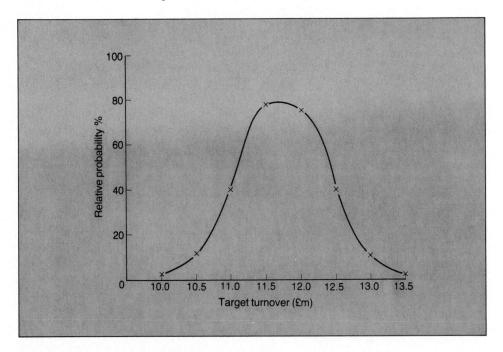

e.g. Turnover *may exceed* £12.5m.
1 Turnover ...................................... £11.5m.
2 Turnover ...................................... fall below £10.5m.
3 Turnover ...................................... to exceed £13.0m.
4 Turnover ...................................... not to drop below £10.0m.
5 Turnover ...................................... only reach £11.0m.
6 Turnover ...................................... even hit £12.5m.

## 5.3.3 Recommendation

| Recommended action | ◄──► | Conclusion/Finding |
|---|---|---|
| *** National advertising must be stopped<br>*** It is strongly recommended that national advertising is/be stopped<br>*** National advertising should be stopped<br>** It is recommended that telephone selling is/be stopped<br>** It is advisable to reduce telephone selling<br>* The appointment of a client relations manager could/might be considered | in view of | the high cost.<br>the poor results.<br>the success of indirect marketing. |

Recommendations: *** = strong  ** = neutral  * = weak

Use the following table to make similar sentences by linking the recommended actions on the left to the conclusions/findings on the right. Each conclusion/finding has three appropriate courses of action.

| Recommended action | Conclusions/Findings |
|---|---|
| a) Commission market research into agricultural equipment buyers **<br>b) Examine feasibility of using our own salesmen **<br>c) Improve after-sales care ***<br>d) Raise rates of commission *<br>e) Increase number of follow-up sales calls ***<br>f) Raise rates of commission *<br>g) Increase salesmen's salaries *<br>h) Investigate competitors' salesmen's salaries **<br>i) Reconsider rates of commission ** | 1 High turnover in sales staff<br><br>2 Loss of existing clients<br><br>3 Low return from foreign agents |

# 5.4 WRITING

## 5.4.1

Rewrite the following report extract under these three headings:
1 *Findings*  2 *Conclusions*  3 *Recommendations*

Our Area Manager in Morlanda has reported
distribution difficulties in the north of the
country, an area affected by floods during the
last few months. There have been 22 truck
breakdowns and these have resulted in complaints

about poor delivery times. On the other hand, there have been no problems with delivery times in the south. In fact, there is evidence that the warehouse there is both overstocked and overmanned. It is obvious that the major geographical differences between the north and the south were not taken into account when planning the distribution network in Morlanda. In view of this, the feasibility of warehousing more goods in the north should be considered. Another problem which the Area Manager has reported is difficulty in obtaining prompt payment for goods delivered. Evidence of this can be found in the annual accounts which indicate that £25,000 was owed at the end of the year. Small customers are largely to blame. In two cases, customers have gone bankrupt and this has resulted in bad debts of £45,000. The Area Manager concludes that this problem will continue as long as the economy is depressed. He suggests that a penalty clause should be included in all delivery contracts.

## 5.4.2

Use your version of the last report extract as a model to write up the following notes into the District Manager's report.

FINDINGS

<u>Production problems</u>

In the east / strikes / 6 stoppages / 20% below production target
In the west / no strikes / 10% above target and overcapacity

<u>Personnel problems</u>

Difficulty in recruitment / personnel budget : £10,000 for job advertisements / low salary rates e.g. maintenance and electrical engineers : only £150 per month basic

## CONCLUSIONS
- differences in working conditions between east and west
- unattractive salaries compared with other local companies

## RECOMMENDATIONS

long term : improvement of working conditions in the east
short term : reduction of production targets in the east
short term : increase in production targets in the west
long term : increase in salaries of technical personnel
long term : improvement in employee benefits

# 6 SUMMARISING

A summary is a short statement of the content of a longer document. It can act as the introduction to a report, as an indication to the reader whether it is of interest or as a time-saver for readers who do not have time to read the whole report.

## 6.1 READING AND UNDERSTANDING

You work for a team of management consultants. You have been asked by your boss to produce a summary of the problems faced by your client, a recruitment agency. Here are the findings of the team who were asked to report on the viability of the company.

1 Read through the following section and decide which two key financial indicators (important financial results) are considered.

---

Finance

In the period 1975-80, annual turnover increased by 75% from £200,000 to £350,000. Since 1980 turnover has fallen by almost 10% to a level of £316,000 at the end of 1982. Profitability during the first period did not show the same rate of increase. Profits rose from £6,000 in 1975 (3% of turnover) to £17,500 in 1980 (5% of turnover). Moreover in the last two years they have fallen dramatically to just £5,500 recorded at the end of 1982.
On the assets side, the company has continued to be undercapitalised with most investment in the above seven year period going to a large advertising budget – 18% of turnover in 1980.
A competitive pricing policy was introduced in 1975 whereby client fees were discounted in 43% of all cases. This was coupled with increased spending on national advertising (an average of £200 per week in 1975 rising to over £1,200 per week in 1980).

---

2 This extract also deals with two other aspects of the company's finances. What are they?
3 What time period does the report consider?
4 There are two phases in this period. What are they?
5 Why has there been little capital investment in the company?
6 What percentage of turnover was spent on national advertising in 1975?
7 Now read the next page of the findings. As you read, note down management and non-management positions.

## Management Structure and Functions

The company has three directors, two of them with no direct day-to-day involvement in the running of the business. The third director, Mr Charles Kitchener, is also the Managing Director. He is responsible for the three major policy areas of the company: finance, sales and personnel. Under him, there is a General Office Manager, responsible for salaries, administration, etc.; an Accounts Manager; a Client Relations Manager; and six Recruitment Managers who deal direct with client companies. The actual recruitment interviews are carried out by six junior recruiters/interviewers. In addition, there is a full-time secretary/receptionist.

There is a monthly Board of Management meeting at which major decisions are taken. Besides the Managing Director, the Office, Accounts and Client Relations Managers and at least one Recruitment Manager must be present at these meetings. It is clear from the minutes that all non-directors have an advisory rather than a decision-making role.

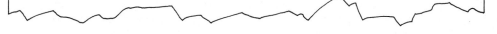

8  What is the ratio of management to non-management staff?
9  What is the minimum number of people present at the Board of Management meeting?
10  Who makes the decisions at these meetings?
11  What are the main areas of policy dealt with in the following extract?

## Promotion

As mentioned above, the MD is ultimately responsible for advertising and sales decisions. However, the six Recruitment Managers have day-to-day responsibility for holding onto existing clients and finding new ones.

The new pricing policy, referred to earlier, was the subject of a major direct marketing campaign in 1975/76. The Recruitment Managers were given the power to discount client fees by a maximum of 30%. It was at the discretion of these managers how much was offered to individual clients. Analysis reveals that 43% of clients were offered discounts, 54% of these the full 30% while the rest varied between 15 and 30%. Prospective clients were also offered discounted rates of 20% for the first year of business. However, in practice many of these new clients continued to pay

less than the advertised fees after the first contract year was
over.
The main means of attracting new clients was the use of national
newspaper advertising which, as has already been shown, expanded
rapidly during the second half of the seventies. The target for
this advertising has always been UK-based companies. The effects
of the recession in the late seventies and early eighties led to a
marked downturn in the number of contracted new clients and the
loss of some existing business. On the other hand, there is
evidence to suggest that many other recruitment agencies have
survived the recession by turning to lucrative foreign markets,
especially the Middle East where recruitment demand remains high.

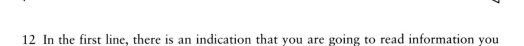

12  In the first line, there is an indication that you are going to read information you
have already seen. What is the expression that indicates this?
13  There are two more cases where information is repeated. What expressions are used
to indicate this repetition?
14  What percentage of clients were paying advertised rates during their first year?
15  What percentage of clients were offered less than a 30% discount?
16  Which external factor contributed to the downturn in business in the early eighties?
17  Now read this final extract and calculate for 1982:
   a) The total salaries and benefits paid to management staff (excluding non-
      working directors and taking an average of Recruitment Managers' Salaries).
   b) The total salaries and benefits paid to non-management staff.
   c) The total commission paid out.

Salary and Benefit Rates


The directors' salaries amounted to £15,000 each in 1982.
In addition, Mr Kitchener was paid a management fee of
£10,000. These salaries kept pace with inflation in the
period 75-80 but were fixed at £15,000 for two years in
1980. If business starts to improve, these salaries will
be raised to match the inflation rate over the last two
years. The General Office and Accounts Managers were paid
£9,000 and £8,500 respectively in 1982. The Client
Relations Manager also received £9,000 but, in addition,
was paid a commission of £5,000 based on client fees.

Basic salaries for the Recruitment Managers were in the
range £6,500 to £8,000 depending on age and experience.
However, on top, all six have benefitted considerably
from the increased rates of commission introduced in
1978. These were increased from 8% to 15% on total client
fees and resulted in an average annual commission per
manager of £8,000 in 1982. It is worth noting that if
this increase had been more moderate, profitability
would have kept pace with the rapid rise in turnover. The
junior recruiters receive a basic salary of £6,000 plus
overtime payments if more than four hours per week are
worked, and travel allowance if they live more than ten
kilometres from the office. These extra payments amount
to an average of £1,000 per annum each. The secretary's
present salary is £5,000.

18  Why were the directors' salaries fixed at £15,000 in 1980?
19  How much was the Accounts Manager paid in 1982?
20  How much is the basic salary for the most senior Recruitment Manager?
21  Why did profitability not keep pace with the rise in turnover?

You have now summarised, in note form, the following main points:

Turnover:       rapid rise followed by decline
Profitability:  gradual rise followed by decline
Advertising     mainly national; rapid increase in costs
Pricing:        big discounts 75–82
Staffing:       ratio 10:7 management to non-management
Decisions:      only MD
Pay:            ratio 4:1 (approx.) management to non-management; large increase in
                commissions

On the basis of these, it is now possible to write two draft summaries:

Summary (draft 1)

After a period of rapid growth between 1975 and 1980, the company
has started to decline. Throughout the past seven years the
company has had low profits. As far as promotion is concerned, the
company has restricted itself to regular national newspaper
advertising and a very competitive pricing policy. On the
personnel front, although there are three more managers than
'workers', decision-making is the Managing Director's sole
responsibility. The pay structure also reveals that the directors

and managerial positions account for about 80% of the salaries and
other benefits.

---

Summary (draft 2)

The poor results of the last two years have, to a great extent,
been due to the failure on the part of the management to recognise
the changing trend in the recruitment business.

   In addition, the discount price policy, which led to a very
significant increase in growth from 1975 to 1980 was offset by the
excessive increases in commission paid to Recruitment Managers.

   The company has a top-heavy management structure which is
accentuated by the very high proportion of salaries and benefits
paid to management.

   As the only working director, Mr Kitchener must be blamed for
the company's decline.

---

22   What features do you notice that make these summaries different? Which summary
is descriptive and which is evaluative?

## 6.2   TASKS

### 6.2.1

Read the following summary of a report on environmental conditions at work. Break it
down into the following parts: (a) Terms of reference, (b) Findings, (c) Conclusions, (d)
Recommendations.

---

In brief, the report sets out to list present conditions on the
shop floor. It draws attention to such features as lighting, dirt,
ventilation, washing and sanitary conditions. Particular
emphasis is placed on the lack of rest facilities for employees.
It concludes that, although working conditions are generally
above average, the company should consider building a separate
rest room for employees.

---

## 6.2.2

Use the information in the extract to complete the flow chart which follows it.

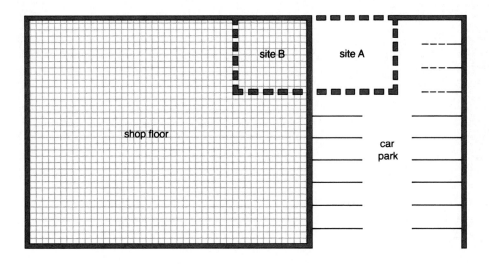

There are difficulties with both sites for the proposed rest facilities. If site A was chosen, this would mean the loss of 30 square metres of parking space. Site B, on the other hand, would involve the use of existing shop-floor space. One advantage of site B is the relative ease of construction whereas site A would involve the digging of new foundations. In both cases the cost will be over £10,000 and probably nearer £15,000 in the case of site A.

Realistic completion dates will be April 83 for site B and August 83 for site A as long as the architects' plans are received within the next two months.

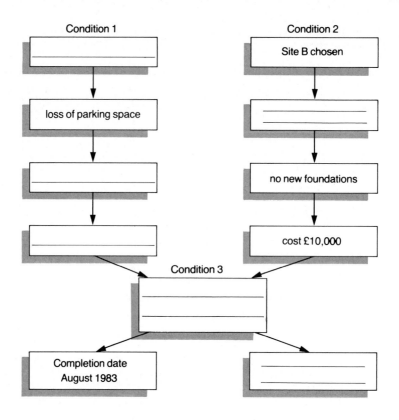

## 6.2.3

Complete the list of 'pros' and 'cons' by reading the following evaluative summary.

The architects' plans and proposals have confirmed that site A would be more expensive and take longer to complete than site B. However, they also pointed to some planning problems with the latter site. Siting the rest facilities on the shop floor would mean that employees would be exposed to continual shop-floor noise whereas this would be considerably reduced in the case of site A. In addition, it would be difficult to ventilate site B while the exterior position of site A would mean improved ventilation. Finally, although site B is closer to the work-place, its size would be limited by the availability of spare space on the shop floor.

| Site B | Pros (+) | Cons (−) |
|--------|----------|----------|
|  | cheaper to construct<br>faster to complete<br>...................................................... | ......................................................<br>......................................................<br>...................................................... |

# 6.3 LANGUAGE PRACTICE

## 6.3.1 Contrast

Look at the following ways of expressing contrast:
a) Turnover increased. *However*, profitability fell.
   *Although* turnover increased, profitability fell.
   Profitability fell *(even) though* turnover increased.
b) It would be difficult to ventilate site B, *while/whereas* the exterior position of site A would improve ventilation.

a) *However* is used for general contrasts where the ideas are not equivalent. *Although* is used when there is a contrast that surprises us. *Even though* is like although but more emphatic.
b) *While/whereas* are used where there is a contrast between equivalent ideas.
Use **although, even though, whereas, while** or **however** to contrast the following:

| | |
|---|---|
| 1  There are only six recruiters. | They do most of the work. |
| 2  Site B would be easy to build on. | Site A would require new foundations. |
| 3  Salaries have been fixed for two years. | They will be revised if business improves. |
| 4  The recruitment agency concentrated on the UK. | Its competitors turned to foreign markets. |
| 5  There are ten managers. | Only the Managing Director has decision-making power. |
| 6  Working conditions are above average. | There is no rest room. |
| 7  The Recruitment Managers received a basic salary of £7,250. | They benefitted from high rates of commission. |
| 8  Prospective clients were offered discounted rates for the first year of business. | Many of these new clients continued to pay less after the first contract year. |
| 9  There are ten managers. | There are only seven non-management staff. |
| 10  Site A will be easy to ventilate. | Site B will be exposed to fumes from the shop floor. |

## 6.3.2 Condition

In the following statements of condition:
a) expresses a universal situation;
b) expresses a possible situation;
c) expresses a hypothetical situation;
d) expresses a hypothetical situation in the past.

| a) | If the junior recruiters *work* more than four hours overtime | they *receive* overtime payments. |
|---|---|---|
| | Present Simple | Present Simple |

| b) | If business *starts* to improve | salaries *will be* increased. |
|---|---|---|
| | Present Simple | Will form |

| c) | If site A *was* chosen | 30 square meters of parking space *would be* lost. |
|---|---|---|
| | Past Simple | Would form |

| d) | If the increase *had been* more moderate | profitability *would have kept* pace with the rise in turnover. |
|---|---|---|
| | Past Perfect | Would Have + Past Participle |

Choose one of methods (a) – (d) to make sentences from the following table:

| Condition | Result |
|---|---|
| 1  The company / advertise / overseas | It / be / more competitive / last year |
| 2  Employees / live / more than 10 km from office | They / receive / travel allowance |
| 3  We / choose / site B | The building / finish / by April |
| 4  Managing Director / resign / now | The company / benefit / immediately |
| 5  The company / pay / less commission | Profits / be / higher / last year |
| 6  We / receive / architects' plans / next week | The building / complete / next April |
| 7  Employees / work / more than 10 hours overtime | They / get / an extra day's holiday |
| 8  He / be / Managing Director | The company / collapse |
| 9  There / be / fewer management staff | More work / do |
| 10  We / not build / rest room | The employees / strike |

## 6.3.3  Addition

We can express the idea of addition as follows:

The recruitment interviews are carried out by six junior recruiters.
*In addition*, there is a full-time secretary.
*Besides* the six junior recruiters, there is (also) a full-time secretary.
There are *not only* six Recruitment Managers, *but also* four other managers.
*Like* the other directors, the Managing Director receives a high salary.
*Moreover* he is paid a management fee of £10,000.

Complete the following passage by inserting appropriate expressions:
To summarise, the company faces several problems. The last two years have shown that
it is ............................. slow to adapt to changing conditions .............................
unwilling to look for new markets. ............................., the management structure of
the company is unsuitable for this kind of business. ............................. the excessive

number of managers, there is the problem of poorly defined responsibilities.
............................, the ratio between salary and commission is out of proportion.


## 6.4  WRITING


### 6.4.1
Complete the summary from the following notes:

**Terms of reference:** report on results of market research survey into consumer demand for rabbit meat in 2 sample areas: N. England and S. England / recommendations for siting and size of new rabbit farm

**Findings:** decline in beef consumption + pork and lamb / growth in chicken consumption / tastes: (southern sample) chicken bland - resistance to rabbit (often a pet); (northern sample) chicken bland - no resistance to rabbit (common dish in past)

**Conclusion:** uncertain market in South, needs promotion; good potential in North, with competitive price v. chicken

**Recommendations:** large factory (economies of scale) near industrial centre in North (eg. Manchester)

Summary of Report on Rabbit Meat Potential

In short, the report sets out to review ......................... .
It draws attention to the decline in consumption of not only
.............. but also ............. and ............. .
Although ............. has now taken over as the principal meat
dish in the UK, the majority of both samples stated that they found
the taste of ........................ . However, there was
considerable ............. to ............. in the
............. where the animal is often kept as a
.............. . In the ............., there was relatively
little .............., as ............. had once been
.............in this area. The report concludes that the market
in southen England would involve ............. whereas, in the
............. , a ........................ would ensure
............. sales. On this basis, it recommends that a
........................ should be sited near an
........................ such as ............. .

## 6.4.2

Now, using the previous summary as a model, write up another summary based on the
following notes:

Terms of reference: to review the results of a market survey into the
demand for foreign language training in small
and medium-sized businesses in the UK

Findings: increase in need for exports to France, Germany
and Spain
medium-sized companies: recognised the
advantage of speaking customers' language / no
money for language training
small businesses: recognised advantage of speaking
customers' language / prepared to spend some
money on French training for salesmen

Conclusions: difficult to sell foreign language training to
medium-sized companies / good potential for
small companies if not too expensive

Recommendations: advertise short intensive courses in French in
local newspapers

# APPENDIX

As an appendix to this course, you will find some additional work on routine writing tasks.

## A  ROUTINE WRITING TASKS

### A.1  Standard personnel reports

These are sometimes called 'Standards of Performance' or 'Personnel Appraisal Forms'. Their purpose is to summarise the performance of employees over a certain period (normally a year) and make recommendations for promotion or career development. They generally include two sections: Strengths (Accomplishments) and Weaknesses.

### A.1.1

Here are some words that are used when writing *positively* about an employee. Classify them under the headings on the left:

| | | | |
|---|---|---|---|
| 1 alertness | a) methodical | 5 control | i) smart |
| | b) tidy | | j) rational |
| 2 analytical ability | c) enterprising | 6 initiative | k) friendly |
| | d) calm | | l) dynamic |
| 3 appearance | e) meticulous | 7 judgement | m) strict |
| | f) co-operative | | n) conscientious |
| 4 application | g) astute | 8 relationships | o) lively |
| | h) industrious | | p) decisive |

### A.1.2

If you want to write *negatively*, you can say: He lacks judgement / She lacks initiative, etc. Or you can use the following words. Classify them under the headings on the left:

| | | | |
|---|---|---|---|
| 1 alertness | a) unsightly | 5 control | i) slack |
| | b) lax | | j) unresponsive |
| 2 analytical ability | c) unresourceful | 6 initiative | k) incompetent |
| | d) untidy | | l) unsociable |
| 3 appearance | e) dull | 7 judgement | m) obscure |
| | f) lenient | | n) lazy |
| 4 application | g) unsystematic | 8 relationships | o) unwise |
| | h) uninterested | | p) interfering |

## A.2 Memos

A memorandum is a written note, usually sent through the internal post. It can serve the following purposes: **reminding; drawing attention** to a situation problem; and **instructing**. It should be brief and to the point. Study this sample memo:

```
Date: 27.2.82                     Ref: AC/CF/521

To: Assistant Accountant          From: Chief Accountant

Subject: Annual Accounts


The Board have fixed the date of the AGM for 30.4.82. Your draft of
the accounts should be ready for submission by 14.3.82
```

Look at 6.2.3 on page 60.
a) You are the Factory Manager. Write a memo to the Personnel Manager drawing attention to the disadvantages of site B.
b) You are the Personnel Manager. Reply to memo (a) and suggest a meeting to discuss the final choice on 16.4.82.
c) You are the Factory Manager. Write a memo to your chief engineer. Ask him to attend the above meeting.

## A.3 Minutes

The minutes are the written record of a meeting. They should record the following:
a) Date and place of meeting.
b) The names of those present.
c) The items of business and the decisions reached (in the same order as the meeting agenda).
They should be a faithful record of the meeting but brief and to the point. Below are some sample minutes of the meeting held to discuss the siting of the rest facilities mentioned in 6.2.2.

```
Minutes of Meeting held to discuss siting of rest
        facilities held at 1400 on 16.4.82


Present:  Site Manager (Chair), Factory Manager,
          Chief Engineer


1  The Minutes of the Meeting held on 15.3.82 were
   read and confirmed as being a true record.
```

2 Matters arising from the Minutes: None

3 Architects' proposals: The Factory Manager
   reported that the choice of site B would mean:
         i) exposure to shop-floor noise;
       ii) poor ventilation;
     iii) limited space.

4 Chief Engineer's report: the Chief Engineer
   confirmed that shop-floor space was limited
   especially in times of high production.

5 Resolved: Final costings and building schedule
   for site A would be requested from the architects.

Next meeting to take place: 14.5.82

Write up the Minutes of the following meeting from this transcript (the Minutes of the previous meeting have just been read):

| Site Manager: | OK, we've all seen the final costings and building schedule for site A. Are there any comments? |
|---|---|
| Chief Engineer: | No, not really. Only I think that the building schedule is a bit optimistic. |
| Factory Manager: | Yes, I thought so too. I'd also like to bring up the problem of car-parking facilities. |
| Site Manager: | I wondered when someone would mention that. I'm afraid there are just going to be fewer parking spaces. The reserved parking for managers will continue but, as for the rest, it will be on a first come, first served basis. |

| | |
|---|---|
| Factory Manager: | That's all very well, but the nearest parking round here is a 20 minute walk. I reckon we're letting ourselves in for a lot of late starts. |
| Site Manager: | I don't see why. They can't have everything. They're getting their new rest facilities. They'll just have to get up a little earlier in the morning. |
| Chief Engineer: | Why don't we investigate the possibility of using some of the spare space on the other side of the road? |
| Site Manager: | You mean the land belonging to Cussins and Sons? |
| Chief Engineer: | Yes, perhaps we could rent it on a short-term basis until they get round to building on it. |
| Site Manager: | That's not a bad idea. George, could you get on to that? You know, approach them and see whether they're interested. You can tell us what their reaction is at the next meeting. |
| Factory Manager: | Sure. Talking of the next meeting, I'm away next month. It'll have to be the end of this month or six weeks from now. |
| Site Manager: | We'd better make it the end of the month. So, we'll put the site A proposals up for final approval from the Board. As soon as we've got that, we can get started on the rest room. Hopefully, next week. |

# B  REPORT ORGANISATION AND STRUCTURE

## B.1  Standard pattern

a) Title page:
    i)  the subject of the report;
    ii)  the writer of the report;
    iii)  the date of the report;
    iv)  the reference number (if any).

b) Table of contents: using the same numbering system as in the report itself.
c) Summary (sometimes called 'Abstract').
d) Terms of reference (sometimes called 'Introduction') saying:
   i) why the report was written;
   ii) who it was written for;
   iii) what its scope and limitations are.
e) Findings ('Main part'): giving the facts and evidence (NB non-essential information should go in the Appendix).
f) Conclusions.
g) Recommendations.
h) Appendix / Appendices (sometimes called 'Annex').
i) Bibliography: giving the names of books, other reports used as references.

## B.2 Approaching the task

The following stages are recommended:
1 Ask yourself: Why have you been chosen to write the report?
               What is the purpose of the report?
               Who is going to read the report?
2 Collect information.
3 Select relevant information.
4 Organise the information: Produce a skeleton plan from Introduction to Recommendations.
               Think about the visuals (graphs, tables, etc.) you will use.
5 Write the first draft: Decide how much needs to be included in the Findings to support Conclusions and Recommendations.
               Decide on the right tone and style.
6 Read through the first draft: Correct, reorganise, add and omit.
7 Write the Summary.
8 Write the final draft.

# KEY

The symbol ►M◄ indicates that the answer given is only a model and that there are other correct versions. Where two words or expressions are equally correct, they are both given with a stroke between them.

## UNIT 1

### 1.1

1 d    2 To get the correct machine for the volume of copies required.    3 Because they have not made proper estimates of the number of copies made.    4 1.25p    5 3.15p    6 b    7 Its position.    8 There were over 8% spoilt copies in June and nearly as many as that the month before.    9 There always seem to be a lot of people waiting.    10 b c d    11 Tax relief.    12 Buying.    13 1.73p    14 b    15 It is necessary to change this type of equipment frequently and used copiers are not easy to sell.    16 The tax situation.    17 It is a way to avoid making payment of tax.    18 b

### 1.2.1

A    1 fact    2 opinion    3 fact    4 fact    5 opinion
B    1 fact    2 opinion    3 fact    4 fact    5 opinion

### 1.2.2

1 imprecise    2 imprecise    3 imprecise    4 Weight: precise    5 Size: precise    6 precise    7 Time for the first copy: precise    8 imprecise

### 1.2.3

a) Large increase in number of local calls by staff.    b) Increase in costs.    c) Complaints from customers.

### 1.3.1

3 The Zenton has a higher output than the Berta, but a lower output than the Arrow. The Arrow has the highest output and the Berta has the lowest output.    4 The Arrow is heavier than the Berta, but lighter than the Zenton. The Zenton is the heaviest and the Berta is the lightest.    5 The Zenton is wider than the Arrow, but narrower than the Berta. The Berta is the widest and the Arrow is the narrowest.    6 The Zen-

ton is more reliable than the Arrow, but less reliable than the Berta. The Berta is the most reliable and the Arrow is the least reliable.

## 1.3.2

1 A report was made in order to assess the relative costs of photocopiers.    2 The training centre was established because of the low level of supervisory knowledge. 3 The report was a failure because of imprecise terms of reference.    4 The training course was cancelled because of low staff attendance.    5 Output went down because of difficult trading conditions.    6 The photocopier was inefficient because of poor maintenance facilities.    7 They leased the machine in order to postpone tax payments.    8 Efficiency was increased because of improved training methods.

## 1.3.3

1 Imprecise terms of reference resulted in / caused an unsatisfactory report.    2 Low demand resulted from / was caused by an expensive product.    3 The high level of leasing resulted from / was caused by a higher level of taxation.    4 Lack of interest in the Suggestion Scheme resulted from / was caused by low staff morale.    5 The success of the report resulted from / was caused by careful planning.    6 The unsuitable photocopy service resulted from / was caused by poor maintenance of equipment.

## 1.4.1

2 The purpose of this report is to investigate the supervisors' training course in order to recommend new methods of training.    3 The purpose of this report is to investigate the relative costs of renting, buying and leasing photocopiers so as to establish the most efficient method.    4 The purpose of this report is to investigate the Company Suggestion Scheme in order to identify problems with the present scheme and recommend a new scheme.    5 The purpose of this report is to investigate staff use of company telephones for private calls so as to assess the scale of this practice.    6 The purpose of this report is to investigate the management trainees' introductory course in order to determine the reasons for the high failure rate and recommend improvements.

# UNIT 2

## 2.1

1 a and b    2 by continent    3 telephone density (telephones per 100 inhabitants)    4 the average relation between GNP and telephone density    5 a, b and d    6 1950    7 1981    8 hoped-for or planned future developments    9 b 10 local calls    11 by dividing revenue by expenditure    12 by dividing revenue by telecommunications manpower    13 by dividing engineering work by engineering manpower    14 a) 1 b) 1 c) 1 and 2 d) 2 and 3    15 fig. 3 to table (this is, of course, debatable)

*2.2.1*

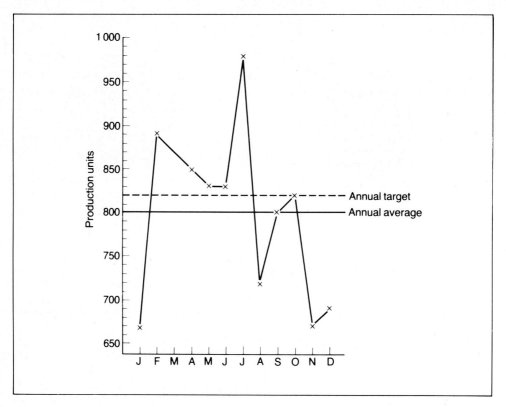

*2.2.2*

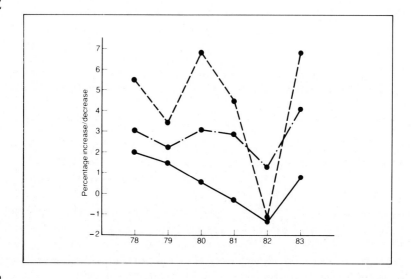

*2.2.3*

There is no right or wrong answer. It is open for discussion.

## 2.2.4

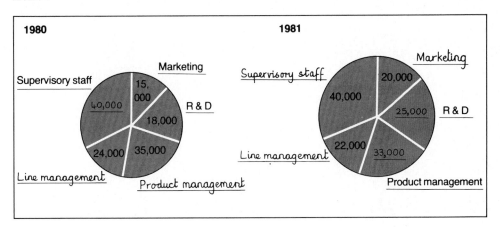

## 2.3.1

1 to     2 of     3 at     4 by     5 at     6 to     7 to     8 at

## 2.3.2

►M◄ 1 because too many     2 since too much     3 as too little     4 since too little     5 because too few     6 as too few

## 2.3.3

►M◄ 1 upward trend     2 rose steadily     3 levelled off     4 increased (again) gradually     5 sudden fall     6 dramatic increase     7 peak

## 2.4.1

above – As can be seen – column – rows – Of particular note

## 2.4.2

Absenteeism has reached its highest level for six years. Three years ago we had an average absentee level of 4%. Despite our proposals, laid down in the second five-year productivity plan, absenteeism has risen to around three hundred workdays lost per year.

A distressing feature of absenteeism here is that only about a hundred of the workdays lost were officially reported, i.e. the absentee telephoned or sent a doctor's note. The other 65% gave no reasons for their absence. We recommend that a new clause be added to the Contract of Employment, Para. 2, page 3:

'Employees who are absent without leave will have their earnings reduced by an amount equivalent to the number of hours lost.'

# UNIT 3

## 3.1

1 d    2 c    3 a    4 b    5 a    6 five new posts    7 producing full job descriptions    8 15 posts    9 internal applicants    10 the external advertisements    11 external advertising    12 the panel interview    13 the case in which the first-choice candidate did not accept the post    14 d    15 a    16 c    17 c    18 c

## 3.2.1

1 f    2 e    3 c    4 b    5 a    6 d

## 3.2.2

1 c and d    2 a and e    3 b

## 3.2.3

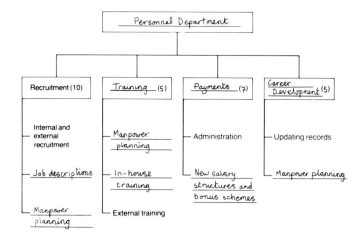

## 3.3.1

1 is headed    2 consists of    3 In addition to    4 consists of    5 not only but also    6 consists of    7 Besides    also

## 3.3.2

is divided – provides – deals – is received – is allocated – carries out – is staffed – work – is appointed – rotates/is rotated – acts

## 3.3.3

1 retirement age    2 career development manager    3 Job agency advertising    4 Internal staff training    5 National newspaper advertising    6 Senior management recommendations    7 Careful material collection    8 Good material selection

## 3.4.1

Heading: *EFFECTS OF SHORTENING THE WORKING WEEK*

1 *IMMEDIATE* effects

*INCREASE IN OVERTIME* → *RISE IN UNIT COSTS*

2 *LONG-TERM* effects

*LESS MOVEMENT* → *LESS FLEXIBILITY* → *LESS EXPERIENCE*

*AND EXCHANGE*

## 3.4.2

receives a complaint from an employee – deals with it himself – takes it to the Works Council – requests a written complaint – it interviews – makes a recommendation to the Board of Directors – discuss the complaint – inform the Works Council of their decision – informs the employee

When – it – He – then – before – it – Having – They – he – He – before – Finally – before

# UNIT 4

## 4.1

The report is organised chronologically.
1 He had been Chief Accountant in the company. 2 For nine months. 3 He considered his main duty was to exert tight financial control. 4 He was most successful at cutting costs. 5 Four (including Mr Gwent). 6 He left because he found it impossible to work with the Finance Director. 7 They could be logically organised. 8 a) formal b) impersonal

## 4.2.1

Personal details: a, j, n, Education: b, e, g, k Qualifications: h, l
Work experience: f, i, o, p Health: c, m Hobbies: d, m

## 4.2.2

a) interest rates – when – how much – ½ – 1½ – under a – over a
b) Mr Field – Mrs Powers

## 4.2.3

1 d 2 c 3 a 4 b

|  | 1 | 2 | 3 | 4 |
|---|---|---|---|---|
| Personal pronouns | X |  |  | X |
| Passives |  |  | X |  |
| Idiomatic phrases | X |  |  |  |
| Expressions of certainty |  | X | X |  |
| Expressions of possibility |  |  |  | X |

## 4.3.1

►M◄ 1 Levels of investment were discussed for several hours.    2 It was felt that investment in the manufacturing sector should be increased.    3 Different opinions were expressed on the subject of trade with China.    4 It was agreed that the advertising budget should be increased by 5%.    5 It was suggested that spending on TV advertising should be doubled.    6 Leaving it at the same level was recommended. 7 There was no agreement about advertising.    8 It was proposed that the matter should be postponed.    9 It was felt that enough time had been spent on this question.    10 It was agreed that more time should be allowed for this question at the next meeting.

## 4.3.2

►M◄ Mr Field felt that the bank's lending policy had to change and that, in the present economic climate, we should be helping more small companies. Mrs Powers agreed but felt that the problem was that small companies were often afraid to approach the banks for a loan. Mr Field disagreed. He said he had met a local businessman recently who was trying to raise capital for investment in new machinery. He had tried the banks and found their terms very unfavourable. Mrs Powers said that she was sure that there were some small firms that would like to borrow from us but that there were many others who wouldn't come near us. She asked whether he had seen the latest borrowing figures. Mr Field said that he hadn't. Mr Keen interrupted here and suggested that we should improve things in two ways. Firstly our image and secondly our actual lending terms.

## 4.3.3

1 retired  had held    2 were  had reached    3 were introduced  had built up
4 had  set up    5 had recovered  stabilised    6 rose  had been    7 had lost
8 was signed  had voted

## 4.4.1

a) *General Financial Control*
Financial results during the year 1981 indicate Mr Hart's ability to reduce costs significantly. This is evidenced by the downward trend in running costs throughout the year. By the end of the year, they had dropped significantly below forecast levels.

b) *Budgetary Control*
Furthermore the Finance Director's budget forecasts for 1982 were considerably lower than other departmental budgets. There is evidence to suggest that Mr Hart's control over departmental budgets was also very rigid. In particular, the Marketing Director complained frequently of difficulty in receiving funds for advertising campaigns.

c) *Staff Relations*
In June 1981, two junior members of the Finance Department resigned and went to work for one of our competitors. In the following month, F. Flynn, the Finance Director's assistant, asked to be moved to another department. He said he could not work any longer with Mr Hart. In November 1981, the Marketing Director resigned saying 'If he stays, I go.' It was understood that he was speaking about the Finance Director.

## 4.4.2

Operating profits in the whole group have increased by 3% to an average of 7%. Non-European subsidiaries showed a rise to 16%. In Europe, the German company's results were much better while severe problems were still faced by our companies in France and the UK.

Industrial disputes have contributed largely to the drop in operating profits in the UK. Internal disputes accounted for £3m while the rest was due to external disputes such as the transport strike in May.

# UNIT 5

## 5.1

1 To find out why Ferton tractor sales in Morlanda have dropped and to recommend action to recapture market share.    2 May and October    3 July    4 b and d    5 a, e, f, g    6 Because sales have developed better for the JDC 80 than for any other tractor.    7 Because JDC 90 sales do not have an upward trend and because promotion should concentrate on the JDC 80.    8 Because they have shown a steady downward trend.    9 a, c, e, f

## 5.2.1

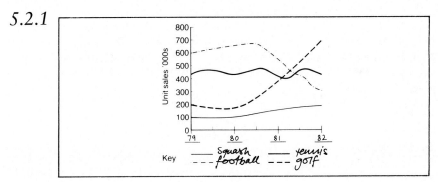

## 5.2.2

1 b and x    2 a and z    3 d and w    4 c and y

## 5.2.3

| Findings | | |
|---|---|---|
| Record of F. Jones, junior salesman: | | |
| | F. Jones | Total (10 salesmen) |
| Repeat business | £ 154,000 | £1,400,000 |
| New clients | £ 75,000 | £550,000 |
| Lost clients | £ 33,000 | £220,000 |

## *5.2.4*

1 Revenue    2 agents    3 Mailshots    4 the telex  the telephone

Appropriate recommendations: 1, 2, 4, 6

## *5.3.1*

▶M◀    1 considerably    2 slightly    3 significant    4 exactly    5 almost
6 slightly    7 noticeable    8 roughly    9 markedly    10 somewhat

## *5.3.2*

▶M◀ 1 is likely to reach    2 probably won't    3 is unlikely    4 is certain
5 might    6 will possibly

## *5.3.3*

▶M◀ a) It is advisable to commission market research into agricultural equipment buyers in view of the loss of existing clients.    b) It is recommended that we examine the feasibility of using our own salesmen in view of the low return from foreign agents. c) Our after-sales care must be improved in view of the loss of existing clients. d) The rates of commission might be raised in view of the high turnover in sales staff. e) The number of follow-up sales calls must be increased in view of the loss of existing clients.    f) Raising the rates of commission might be considered in view of the low return from foreign agents.    g) Salesmen's salaries might be increased in view of the high turnover in sales staff.    h) It is advisable to investigate competitors' salesmen's salaries in view of the high turnover in sales staff.    i) It is recommended that rates of commission be reconsidered in view of the low return from foreign agents.

## *5.4.1*

▶M◀ 1 *Findings*
Distribution difficulties
Our Area Manager in Morlanda has reported distribution difficulties in the north of the country, an area affected by floods during the last few months. There have been 22 truck breakdowns and these have resulted in complaints about poor delivery times. On the other hand, there have been no problems with delivery times in the south. In fact, there is evidence that the warehouse there is both overstocked and overmanned.
Payments
Another problem which the Area Manager has reported is difficulty in obtaining prompt payment for goods delivered. Evidence of this can be found in the annual accounts which indicate that £25,000 was owed at the end of the year. Small customers are largely to blame. In two cases, customers have gone bankrupt and this has resulted in bad debts of £45,000.

2 *Conclusions*
The Area Manager concludes:
– The major geographical differences between the north and the south were not taken into account when planning the distribution network in Morlanda.
– The problem of late payments will continue as long as the economy is depressed.

3 *Recommendations*

He recommends:
– The feasibility of warehousing more goods in the north should be considered.
– A penalty clause should be included in all delivery contracts.

## 5.4.2

▶M◀ 1 *Findings*

Production problems

The District Manager in Morlanda has reported production problems in the east of the country, an area which has been affected by strikes during the last few months. There have been six stoppages and these have resulted in production falling 20% below target. On the other hand, there have been no strikes in the west. In fact, there is evidence that the factory has overcapacity since they were 10% above target.

Personnel problems

He also reports difficulty in recruitment. Evidence of this can be found in the personnel budget in which £10,000 was allocated for job advertisements. Low salary rates are largely to blame. For example, maintenance and electrical engineers are only paid £150 per month basic.

2 *Conclusions*

The District Manager concludes:
– the differences between the east and the west were not taken into account when setting production targets.
– the problem of recruitment will continue as long as the company offers unattractive salaries compared with other local companies.

3 *Recommendations*

He recommends the following action:
Short term:
– production targets in the east should be reduced.
– production targets in the west should be increased.
Long term:
– working conditions in the east should be improved.
– an increase in salaries for technical personnel might be considered.
– employees benefits should be improved.

## UNIT 6

### 6.1

1 turnover and profitability    2 capitalisation and pricing policy    3 1975–82
4 1975–80 and 1981–82    5 Because most investment has gone into the advertising budget.    6 5.2%    7 Managing Director, General Office Manager, Accounts Manager, Client Relations Manager, six Recruitment Managers; six recruiters/interviewers and one secretary/receptionist.    8 10:7    9 five    10 the Managing Director    11 advertising and sales (pricing)    12 'As mentioned above'    13 'referred to earlier' and 'as has already been shown'    14 57%    15 19.78%
16 the recession    17 a) £148,000 b) £47,000 c) £53,000    18 Because busi-

ness was poor.     19 £8,500     20 £8,000     21 Because of the increased rates of commission introduced in 1978.     22 Draft 1 is descriptive. Draft 2 is evaluative (notice use of evaluative statements e.g. 'excessive', 'top-heavy', etc.).

## 6.2.1

a) To list present conditions on the shop floor.     b) Information about lighting, dirt, ventilation, washing and sanitary conditions and, in particular, (the lack of) rest facilities for employees.     c) Working conditions are generally above average. d) The company should consider building a rest room for employees.

## 6.2.2

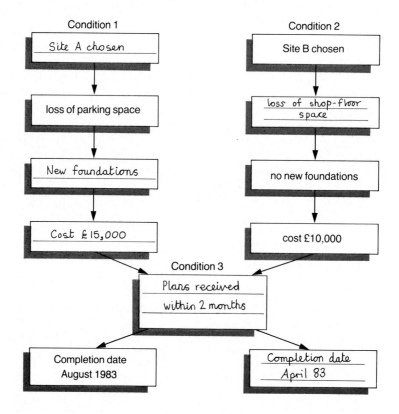

## 6.2.3

| Site B | Pros | Cons |
|---|---|---|
| | cheaper to construct | exposure to noise |
| | faster to complete | difficult to ventilate |
| | Closer to work-place | limited size |

## 6.3.1

▶M◀ 1 Although there are only six recruiters, they do most of the work. 2 Site B would be easy to build on, while site A would require new foundations. 3 Salaries have been fixed for two years. However, they will be revised if business improves. 4 The recruitment agency concentrated on the UK, whereas its competitors turned to foreign markets. 5 Although there are ten managers, only the Managing Director has decision-making power. 6 Working conditions are above average. However, there is no rest room. 7 The Recruitment Managers received a basic salary of £7,250 even though they benefitted from high rates of commission. 8 Although prospective clients were offered discounted rates for the first year of business, many of these new clients continued to pay less after the first contract year. 9 There are ten managers whereas there are only seven non-management staff. 10 Site A will be easy to ventilate, whereas site B will be exposed to fumes from the shop floor.

## 6.3.2

▶M◀ 1 If the company had advertised overseas, it would have been more competitive last year. 2 If employees live more than ten kilometres from the office, they receive a travel allowance. 3 If we chose site B, the building would be finished by April. 4 If the Managing Director resigns now, the company will benefit immediately. 5 If the company had paid less commission, profits would have been higher last year. 6 If we receive the architects' plans next week, the building will be completed next April. 7 If employees work more than ten hours overtime, they get an extra day's holiday. 8 If he had been Managing Director, the company would have collapsed. 9 If there were fewer management staff, more work would be done. 10 If we don't build a rest room, the employees will strike.

## 6.3.3

not only – but also – In addition – Besides – Moreover

## 6.4.1

▶M◀ consumer demand for rabbit meat in two sample areas in England – beef – pork – lamb – chicken – chicken bland – resistance – (eating) rabbit meat – south – pet – north – resistance – rabbit meat – common – promotion – north – competitive pricing policy – good – large factory – industrial centre – Manchester

## 6.4.2

▶M◀ In short, the report sets out to review the results of a market survey into the demand for foreign language training in small and medium-sized businesses in the UK. It draws attention to the increase in the need for exports to France, Germany and Spain. Medium-sized companies recognised the advantage of speaking the customers' language. However, there was no money available for language training. Small businesses both recognised the advantage of speaking the customers' language and were prepared to spend some money on French training for salesmen. The report concludes that, while it would be difficult to sell foreign language training to medium-sized companies, there is a good potential market in small companies if the training is not too expensive. It recommends that short intensive courses in French should be advertised in local newspapers.

# APPENDIX

*A.1.1*   1 l, o   2 e, j   3 b, i   4 h, n   5 d, m   6 c, p   7 a, g   8 f, k

*A.1.2*   1 e, h   2 g, m   3 a, d   4 b, n   5 f, i   6 c, j   7 k, o   8 l, p

## A.2

▶M◀   a)

> Date: 31.3.82
> To: Personnel Manager     From: Factory Manager
> Subject: Siting of rest facilities
> Before we make the final decision about where to put the rest room, I'd like to draw your attention to the disadvantages of site B. Rest would be difficult there because of the noise; the room would be difficult to ventilate adequately; and it would be smaller than if built on site A.

b)

> Date: 4.4.82
> To: Factory Manager     From: Personnel Manager
> Subject: Meeting on siting of rest facilities
> In view of your memo on the disadvantages of site B, perhaps you could attend the next planning meeting. I suggest 16 April at 14 00. Let me know if that is not convenient.

c)

> Date: 6.4.82
> To: Chief Engineer     From: Factory Manager
> Subject: Meeting on siting of rest facilities
> There's a meeting on 16 April at 14 00 to discuss the final choice of the rest room site. Could you make sure that you're free then so that you can attend it with me.

## A.3

▶M◀

> Minutes of Meeting held to discuss rest facilities plans held at 14 00 on 14.5.82
>
> Present: Site Manager (Chair), Factory Manager, Chief Engineer
>
> 1   The Minutes of the Meeting held on 16.4.82 were read and confirmed as being a true record.
> 2   Matters arising from the Minutes: The architects' proposals had been received and were generally acceptable. However, it was felt that the schedule was a little optimistic.
> 3   Parking: Building the rest room on site A would mean a reduction in the number of parking spaces. Alternative facilities were discussed.
> 4   Resolved: The Factory Manager would contact Cussins and Sons with a view to renting parking space opposite the factory on a short-term basis.
> Next meeting to take place: 28.5.82

# GLOSSARY

This contains difficult words and expressions from the report extracts. The page number of the first appearance of the word is given followed by a short explanation. Note that the meanings given are correct for the context in which the word is found. In some cases, there will be other meanings.

*absenteeism* (p.26) the practice of employees staying away from work
*accentuate* (p.58) to emphasise, highlight
*accept* (p.28) to take, agree to receive
*accountant* (p.37) a person specialised in keeping and analysing business accounts
*achieve* (p.46) to reach (a goal, target, etc.)
*actual* (p.17) real
*adapt* (p.62) to make the necessary change for a new situation
*advantage* (p.9) something useful, good
*advisory* (p.55) having the power to advise, recommend
*after sales* (p.46) following the sale
*agenda* (p.66) order of business at a meeting
*aggressive* (p.44) attacking, strong
*alarming* (p.37) very worrying
*alertness* (p.65) being awake and watchful
*allocate* (p.21) to give an employee a clear task, responsibility
*allowance* (p.57) an amount of money allowed for certain expenses
*ambition* (p.30) a strong desire to do something or to succeed
*analytical* (p.65) able to analyse, see clearly
*appearance* (p.65) the way someone looks
*application* (p.28) a form on which you apply for a job
*application* (p.65) effort and attention (to work)
*appoint* (p.37) to give someone a job
*approach* (p.41) to go to see someone and usually request something
*approve* (p.37) to agree to, to think something is satisfactory
*assess* (p.8) to consider and evaluate
*assets* (p.9) all things owned by a company
*astute* (p.65) clever, quick to see an advantage
*attendance* (p.10) being present at a meeting, course, etc.
*availability* (p.60) possibility of being used
*avoid* (p.9) escape, get away from (paying tax, etc.)
*axis* (p.16) horizontal or vertical reference line on a graph

*backlog* (p.19) a build-up of undelivered goods, orders
*bad debts* (p.52) money owed which is never likely to be paid
*balance sheet* (p.9) a written account of assets and liabilities of a company
*bankrupt* (p.52) not able to trade because of excessive debts
*base year* (p.26) a year with which statistics for later years can be compared
*benefit* (p.58) money paid to an employee in addition to salary
*bill* (p.12) an invoice, statement of money owed for service or goods

*billing*  (p.6)  invoicing
*binding*  (p.31)  not able to be broken (of a contract)
*bland*  (p.63)  tasteless
*block*  (p.7)  to stop, prevent
*bonus*  (p.32)  an additional payment for good work, etc. (often at Christmas)
*boost*  (p.46)  to increase
*borrow*  (p.41)  to get money on the understanding that it is repaid
*breach*  (p.31)  a failure to keep to the terms of a contract
*break*  (p.19)  a pause, holiday
*break down*  (p.7)  to stop working due to a fault
*breakdown*  (p.51)  a mechanical fault causing a machine to stop
*broken line*  (p.17)  – – – – – –
*budgetary*  (p.37)  concerning a budget

*calm*  (p.65)  not excited, quiet
*campaign*  (p.44)  a planned operation with a particular aim, target
*candidate*  (p.27)  a person being considered for a job
*capacity*  (p.19)  the quantity of products which can be produced by a factory
*capital cost*  (p.6)  the cost of the machine itself rather than the service, etc.
*capture*  (p.20)  to take (often away from competitors)
*career*  (p.32)  the progression of an employee in a certain profession or job
*cash*  (p.9)  money available immediately
*catch up*  (p.17)  to get level with
*channel*  (p.48)  a means of communication (e.g. telephone)
*chat*  (p.36)  an informal conversation
*check-up*  (p.31)  a session with a doctor in which he or she checks your general health
*clause*  (p.26)  a paragraph in a contract about a particular condition
*clarify*  (p.31)  to make clear
*cold-contact*  (p.46)  not having any previous contact or introduction
*commission*  (p.56)  money paid to the seller related to the amount sold
*compact*  (p.11)  small and neat
*comparative*  (p.44)  measured by comparing
*compensate*  (p.21)  to make a suitable payment for loss or injury
*competitor*  (p.43)  a company which is in the same market
*completion*  (p.59)  finishing
*confidence*  (p.11)  trust
*confine*  (p.35)  to limit, restrict
*conscientious*  (p.65)  having a sense of duty, hard-working and thorough
*consistently*  (p.45)  all the time
*consumption*  (p.63)  the act of buying, consuming
*co-operative*  (p.65)  helpful to other people
*cost-effective*  (p.48)  producing a good profit for the expense/cost
*couple with*  (p.54)  to put together with
*cover*  (p.7)  to include, to be true for
*currency*  (p.31)  the money of a particular country e.g. Germany – DM
*current costs*  (p.37)  day-to-day costs
*cut*  (p.27)  to reduce, to lower

*deal with*  (p.55)  to handle, to have something to do with
*decisive*  (p.65)  able to make decisions quickly
*delay*  (p.28)  to make something happen later than expected
*delivery*  (p.52)  transport of ordered goods to customer
*demand*  (p.19)  the amount of goods and services required by consumers
*direct selling*  (p.44)  selling through direct contact with the potential customer
*disadvantage*  (p.7)  something bad or unfavourable
*discount*  (p.55)  to reduce prices as a special offer to customers
*discretion*  (p.55)  freedom to do what seems best
*dispute*  (p.19)  disagreement between management and workers / may be a strike
*distressing*  (p.26)  causing worry, upsetting
*distribution network*  (p.52)  organisation of places of supply in a region
*distribution outlets*  (p.46)  places (e.g. shops) from which goods can be distributed
*dog*  (p.19)  to be hindered by problems
*dull*  (p.65)  uninteresting
*dynamic*  (p.65)  full of energy

*economical*  (p.11)  good value for money
*efficiency*  (p.7)  the ability to work well
*enterprising*  (p.65)  having initiative and willing to face problems
*essential*  (p.6)  very important
*establish*  (p.6)  to find out
*estimate*  (p.6)  a calculated approximation
*exceed*  (p.19)  to be higher than a certain limit/maximum
*excluding*  (p.8)  not including
*exert*  (p.37)  to put into action
*expansion*  (p.45)  getting bigger
*expenditure*  (p.21)  spending
*experience*  (p.35)  knowledge gained through practice (e.g. a job)
*exposed to*  (p.60)  open to
*external*  (p.27)  outside

*facilities*  (p.8)  aids, equipment and services
*factor*  (p.15)  a consideration, something which must be taken into account
*failure*  (p.11)  not a success
*faithful*  (p.66)  accurate, not changed
*feature*  (p.58)  characteristic
*fee*  (p.54)  money charged usually for a service
*figures*  (p.21)  financial results
*files*  (p.26)  containers of information for reference purposes
*fix*  (p.56)  to set so that something cannot move
*fixed costs*  (p.37)  costs which do not change according to production e.g. rent for a
   building
*floods*  (p.51)  great quantity of water due to heavy rainfall, etc.
*forecast*  (p.15)  a prediction about the future
*formula*  (p.7)  a calculation which produces an answer e.g. $E = MC^2$
*foundation*  (p.59)  the base of a building
*funds*  (p.37)  reserves of money

*get somewhere*  (p.38)  to progress, advance
*GNP*  (p.15)  abbr. Gross National Product

*goods*  (p.52)  products for sale
*guidelines*  (p.11)  advice on certain lines of action

*harvest*  (p.44)  cutting of crops e.g. corn (usually in summer months)
*horizontal*  (p.16)  across, 90° to the vertical
*HQ*  (p.6)  abbr. headquarters i.e. principal office

*identical*  (p.43)  exactly the same
*illustrate*  (p.26)  to show, usually with a picture/diagram
*image*  (p.41)  appearance to the outside world
*implement*  (p.32)  to put into action
*improve*  (p.9)  to get or make better
*incompetent*  (p.65)  not able to do things well/efficiently
*indicator*  (p.54)  a sign of how well a company is doing
*industrious*  (p.65)  hard working
*influence*  (p.15)  to have an effect on something
*initiative*  (p.65)  ability to see what needs to be done and to take action
*inoculation*  (p.31)  injection against disease
*in-service*  (p.20)  during work
*interest rates*  (p.38)  the amount of money (%) a borrower must repay to a lender in
    addition to the sum originally borrowed
*interfering*  (p.65)  getting involved in other people's business
*interim*  (p.30)  the time between two events
*investigate*  (p.6)  to examine/research

*job agency*  (p.27)  a private company which finds employees for employers
*job description*  (p.27)  a summary of the main duties/responsibilities of an employee
*judgement*  (p.65)  quality of judging, assessing

*keep pace with*  (p.57)  to keep at the same speed as
*key*  (p.54)  main

*labour costs*  (p.35)  the costs of employing e.g. salaries, etc.
*lay down*  (p.26)  (of a proposal) to make or write
*lax*  (p.65)  not strict about discipline
*lazy*  (p.65)  not liking hard work
*lease*  (p.6)  to have the right to use a piece of equipment for a fixed number of years
    in return for monthly payments
*leave*  (p.26)  permission
*lend*  (p.41)  to give money on the understanding it will be repaid
*lenient*  (p.65)  not hard especially about discipline
*lightweight*  (p.11)  light, not heavy
*limit*  (p.60)  restrict
*line*  (p.12)  telephone line/connection
*line management*  (p.21)  responsible for the main product, service, operation of a
    company
*lines of communication*  (p.31)  reporting structure and organisation in a company
*lively*  (p.65)  active, interested and awake
*load*  (p.11)  to fill, to put in material ready for use
*loan*  (p.41)  a sum of money which is lent
*lucrative*  (p.56)  profitable

*maintain* (p.20) to keep on, continue at the same level
*maintenance* (p.8) keeping in good condition and repair
*man hour* (p.29) a measurement of what an employee is capable of doing in one hour
*manpower* (p.32) the work force, employees
*market share* (p.20) % of the market held by one company, product, etc.
*matters arising* (p.67) questions or problems left over from the last meeting
*methodical* (p.65) able to do things in an orderly way
*meticulous* (p.65) giving, showing great attention to detail
*minutes* (p.55) written record of a meeting
*miss a golden opportunity* (p.39) not to take advantage of a very good chance
*morale* (p.11) spirit, state of mind of people

*notice* (p.36) warning that you are going to leave a job

*obscure* (p.65) not easily understood
*offer* (p.28) to give something if it is desired
*offset* (p.58) to balance against
*operating profit* (p.42) the amount by which the gross profit is bigger than the operating expenses or overheads
*optimistic* (p.67) expecting the best, confident
*order* (p.19) a request for delivery of goods
*overall* (p.11) total
*overmanned* (p.52) having too many employees
*overstocked* (p.52) having too many goods in stock
*overtime* (p.35) work done outside normal working hours
*owe* (p.52) to be in debt

*panel* (p.27) three or four people sitting together to ask or answer questions
*penalty* (p.52) punishment (usually financial) for failure to keep to an agreement
*pension* (p.32) money received after retirement
*performance* (p.37) achievement and behaviour
*pessimistic* (p.37) expecting the worst
*plans* (p.59) drawings for a design of a building
*PLC* (p.43) abbr. Public Limited Company
*plot* (p.17) to mark a point on a graph
*plough* (p.44) to dig a field before planting
*policy* (p.9) agreed line of action
*post* (p.28) a job
*postpone* (p.9) to put to a later date than planned
*potential* (p.30) possible
*practice* (p.55) reality, not theory
*predecessor* (p.37) a person who held a position before someone else
*predict* (p.15) to estimate for the future
*pricing* (p.46) setting or fixing prices
*procedure* (p.27) a fixed sequence of events or actions
*product management* (p.21) management of particular products
*production unit* (p.35) an item of production, may be the finished product
*productive* (p.48) giving a return for investment, profitable
*productivity* (p.15) the relation between the amount that is produced and the cost of producing it

*profitability* (p.37) the power of a business to earn profits

*profits* (p.54) the difference between income and expenses

*promotion* (p.30) an increase in the position and responsibility of an employee

*promotion* (p.44) activities e.g. advertising, designed to increase the demand for a product

*prompt* (p.52) on time

*proportion* (p.63) out of — : the wrong ratio, too much on one side

*prospects* (p.44) the possibility of getting more business

*purchase* (p.6) buying

*qualifications* (p.38) examinations passed e.g. diplomas

*raise* (p.41) to try to get money

*raise* (p.56) to increase

*range* (p.6) the variation between two limits i.e. large to small, expensive to cheap, etc.

*rate* (p.8) amount, quantity

*rational* (p.65) thinking and logical, not emotional

*realise* (p.44) to achieve

*recapture* (p.43) to win back

*recession* (p.56) a time of economic difficulties

*recommendation* (p.6) definite suggestion or advice

*record* (p.30) report on quality of work

*recruitment* (p.27) process of employing more people in a company

*reduction* (p.37) a lowering or a cut in prices, etc.

*redundant* (p.26) no longer needed; to make somebody — : to dismiss because of lack of work

*reference* (p.27) an opinion of somebody's value (often given by past employers)

*register* (p.12) to record on a meter

*reject* (p.28) to fail, not accept

*relationship* (p.65) the personal connection between two people

*reliable* (p.15) able to be trusted, does not break down

*renew* (p.44) to start again, to sign again

*rent* (p.6) to pay money for the temporary use of equipment

*rental* (p.8) the amount of money paid to rent something

*reserve* (p.28) the person who will substitute for somebody if they are ill, etc.

*resign* (p.37) to leave a job because you want to

*resistance* (p.63) feeling against something

*resolve* (p.67) to decide

*respectively* (p.21) in the order mentioned before

*responsibility* (p.31) duty, particular jobs or tasks

*results* (p.46) financial figures e.g. profits, turnover, etc.

*retirement* (p.28) act of leaving a job usually at the age of 65

*return* (p.48) the profit you receive from an investment

*reverse* (p.46) to make something go in the opposite direction

*review* (p.19) to give a presentation about

*running* (p.55) the management (of a business)

*running costs* (p.8) overhead costs which are common to the products or services of a company

*salary* (p.32) monthly earnings/income of an employee

*seasonal*   (p.43)   according to the seasons e.g. winter, summer
*sector*   (p.15)   a part (of a market)
*service*   (p.8)   regular maintenance checks
*settle*   (p.31)   to find the solution to
*sheet handling*   (p.11)   use of the copy paper facilities
*shop floor*   (p.58)   the factory floor
*shorten*   (p.27)   to make shorter
*short-listed*   (p.27)   having been chosen from a large number of candidates, now only
      three or four candidates
*site*   (p.59)   location
*slack*   (p.65)   lazy, not hard working
*solid line*   (p.16)   _____
*sort*   (p.29)   to arrange in groups, to separate one kind from another
*spoilt*   (p.7)   damaged
*sponsorship*   (p.46)   financial support in return for advertising
*staff*   (p.31)   personnel, employees
*standards of performance (SOPs)*   (p.30)   personnel records, assessments of perform-
      ance
*stock levels*   (p.44)   amount of products, goods in store
*stress*   (p.44)   to emphasise
*strict*   (p.65)   demanding discipline
*stylish*   (p.11)   having style, well designed
*submit*   (p.30)   to send, hand over
*subsidiary*   (p.42)   a company of which more than 50% of the share capital is owned
      by a parent company
*subsidy*   (p.43)   money given by the government to help producers (often to prevent
      them making a loss)
*suitability*   (p.7)   being right for the purpose
*superior*   (p.28)   someone more senior in a company
*supply*   (p.19)   the provision of goods and services by the seller
*survive*   (p.56)   to live through or stay alive in a difficult period

*target*   (p.19)   the specific figure (of sales, etc.) which is aimed for
*tax relief*   (p.8)   reduction in tax owed
*terms*   (p.31)   conditions of a contract, agreement
*tidy*   (p.65)   neat, organised
*tight*   (p.37)   strict, watchful
*trunk call*   (p.18)   long-distance telephone call
*turnover*   (p.54)   the total value of business done in a certain period, usually total
      sales

*ultimately*   (p.55)   in the end, finally
*undercapitalised*   (p.54)   not having enough share capital for the amount of turnover
*unreliable*   (p.7)   cannot be trusted to work well/efficiently
*unresourceful*   (p.65)   having no initiative
*unresponsive*   (p.65)   not reacting quickly
*unsightly*   (p.65)   of poor or unpleasant appearance
*unsociable*   (p.65)   not liking to mix with other people
*unsystematic*   (p.65)   not having a system or logic
*untidy*   (p.65)   not neat or organised
*unwise*   (p.65)   stupid, not clever

# Glossary

*update*  (p.32)  to bring up to date, to modernise

*vacancy*  (p.28)  a free position/job in a company which must be filled
*vertical*  (p.16)  upwards, 90° to the horizontal
*viability*  (p.54)  capability to survive and make profit

*wage*  (p.32)  weekly earnings/income of an employee
*warehouse*  (p.52)  a building where goods are kept before being distributed
*waste*  (p.39)  to use unnecessarily
*workload*  (p.21)  amount of work a person has
*work sheet*  (p.36)  a daily or weekly record of work done